"It *Can't* Happen to Me"

HOW TO
OVERCOME
99
OF LIFE'S MOST
DISTRESSING
PROBLEMS

"It <u>Can't</u> Happen to Me"

HOW TO OVERCOME
99
OF LIFE'S MOST DISTRESSING PROBLEMS

Sam Klarreich, Ph.D.

BRUNNER/MAZEL, *Publishers* • NEW YORK

Library of Congress Cataloging-in-Publication Data
Klarreich, Samuel H.
    "It can't happen to me" : how to overcome 99 of life's most
distressing problems / Samuel H. Klarreich.
        p.   cm.
    Includes bibliographical references.
    ISBN 0-87630-621-0
    1. Adjustment (Psychology)   2. Adjustment (Psychology)—Case
studies.   3. Self-actualization (Psychology)   I. Title.
BF335.K585   1991
158'.12—dc20   91-30005
                                                                    CIP

Published by
BRUNNER/MAZEL, INC.
19 Union Square West
New York, New York 10003

Manufactured in the United States of America

10 9 8 7 6 5 4 3 2 1

Eugene: You feasted on life.

Kasper: Fate dealt you an unfortunate blow.

Regina: You let the dusk come a bit too soon.

Kimi: Such determination in such a small package.

Yetta & Josef: Life is a gift, enjoy it to the fullest.

Florence, Leanne, Rochelle, Lesley: You enrich my life.

Keesha & Kasey: Two magnificent presents.

Warner, Rosemarie and my friends:
Committed to making a difference.

And especially,
Penny: My shining light.

Contents

Part 2: ON THE HOME FRONT

Part 3: ON THE PERSONAL FRONT

Acknowledgments

To Dr. Albert Ellis, one of the most renowned and prolific psychologists of our time—no matter what I write, your profound influence remains.

I wish to gratefully acknowledge the significant contributions of the following health professionals who carefully assisted in collecting the valuable interview data:

C. ABERIN	M. GUDGEON
E. ANTRAM	L. HADER
N. ATAULLAH-JAN	N. HAMMETT
S. BARAN-DMYTRYSHYN	S. KELLY
M. BLAIR	M. MCKEOWN
W. COHRS	C. OLDE
L. DELL'ANNO	V. PARK
R. DELLOSO	R. PONCE
F. DEROCHE	U. REMPEL
E. DEVERA	M. RIDDELL
M. DORAN	L. SAVIDGE
J. DRAPER	P. SHERWOOD
D. ERICKSON	R. SPARKMAN
P. FAIR	R. STAPLES
D. FAWCETT	H. WALTON
S. FEARON	R. WEST
M. GAUCI	L. WILKES
J. GOLDIE	L. WONG
L. GORDON	

To Mark Tracten, Natalie Gilman, and Suzi Tucker of Brunner/Mazel—your support, guidance, enthusiasm, professionalism, and commitment were essential ingredients in the completion of this book. You are truly a credit to your profession.

Introduction _____

WHY READ THIS BOOK? _____

Have you ever wondered why certain people seem to have fewer problems than others?

Have you ever wondered why certain people seem to become less ill than others?

Have you ever wondered why certain people seem to live happier and healthier lives?

Have you ever wondered why certain people manage adversity so well that they seem to create miracles for themselves?

A very common characteristic among these people, whom we'll call "miracle makers," is outlook. Outlook simply means your view of the world, your ideas about what is going on, and the way you think. The thinking of "miracle makers" seems to be marked by optimism, patience, tolerance, and flexibility, combined with a strong dose of humor. Miracle makers have a mental outlook that puts them in a position of power and tremendous control over their own lives. They harness the positive energies of their minds.

I'm very excited about what the mind can potentially do. The mind can influence how we feel, how our body reacts to various events, how we deal with people, and how successful we are on the job. The mind is a very strong force upon which we really have not effectively capitalized. I wrote this book to discover those mental activities that help us to be happier, healthier, and more productive. What better way to accomplish this than to interview people who have overcome adversity—who have made their own miracles.

It is not my intention in this book to minimize what people go through when they first encounter adversity. Intense shock, extreme disbelief, overwhelming numbness, sudden and peculiar disorientation, consuming pain, unforeseeable panic, unprecedented exhaustion—they are all very real and powerful responses to adversity, responses that may vary in terms of intensity and duration. I fully acknowledge these normal emotions. Not long ago, a series of dramatic events occurred in my own life over a short period of time: my favorite uncle passed away; my father-in-law passed away; my mother passed away; my dogs passed away; I helped my father move into a retirement apartment; and my mother-in-law began to experience serious health problems. I, too, fell prey to all of the feelings that were just described.

It is my intention to reveal what it means to make miracles—to create the best quality of life possible under adverse conditions. It is my intention to take the mystery out of the "some-people-have-all-of-the-luck" syndrome, to demonstrate how we all have the ability to turn things around in times of trouble.

THE POWER OF THE MIND

In the 1960s scientists and practitioners began to experiment with a procedure called biofeedback. A number of different machines, when hooked up to various parts of our bodies, helped us to gain control over such functions as heart rate, blood pressure, and brain activity. The reason biofeedback was so useful was that it capitalized on the "powers of the mind." Our minds exerted control over our bodies in the form of reducing heart rate, lowering blood pressure, and modulating brain-wave activity. The biofeedback machines told us in the form of signals such as number readings and various auditory tones whether we were doing a good job.

Placebos offer another example of the power of the mind. People can ingest a pill with the belief that it is going to have an impact on their body. And just because they think this way, certain changes may in fact begin to occur. A person may begin to relax more, become less anxious, become less fearful, and sleep better.

If you are told that you are drinking an alcoholic beverage even if there really is no alcohol, you will probably still experience some side effects. Certain changes may take place in your body. Some people have been known to become a bit giddier, others may become a little rowdier; some people get more aggressive, some become less inhibited, and others become sexually aroused. All of this because we thought that we were consuming something that really was not there. The power of the mind.

Hypnosis refers to an altered state of consciousness, and it too involves the power of the mind. We use hypnosis to manage pain, to overcome fears, to contain anxiety, and to relax. Simply speaking, we are taught through the use of mental pictures and/or mental suggestions to relieve certain hardships and to enhance certain internal strengths.

Did you know that many people with terminal cancer outlive medical predictions. With a particular outlook and a particular way of thinking certain patients have been able to live well beyond medical prognoses and expectations. What is the difference between these patients and those who do not survive? *Thinking.* It seems that certain thinking can heal, extend life, contribute to greater control, harness strength and energy, and allow one to live longer and happier.

Norman Cousins, an author and professor at the University of California School of Medicine, Los Angeles, has pointed out that as individuals we do not have to yield to pain and to the ravages of illness. Here was a man who helped himself overcome a major degenerative illness not only through experimental medical treatment, but also through humor, optimism and hopeful thinking. Cousins has even declared that the minute patients are "diagnosed," their physical condition seems to decline almost immediately. The decline does not necessarily have to do only with the illness, but more with their psychological makeup. Because they have begun to think in very cynical, negative, helpless, and hopeless ways, their physical condition begins to deteriorate very rapidly. If patients were to defy diagnoses and instead regard illnesses, and their associated problems, hardships, and adversities, as challenges to living rather than death sentences, then their physical condition might improve. Cousins, in fact, points out that patients who live beyond the time that their doctors designate usually share the will to go on, resist the diagnoses, and resent the sometimes pessimistic attitudes of the medical community.

Do you know that certain people with sufficiently "strong minds" can actually postpone death for special occasions; that is, these people can will themselves to live long enough to experience an important event. For example, actuaries in California noticed that among the Jewish people, the mortality rate before Passover, a high holiday, was lower, whereas after the holiday, the rate dramatically increased.

It is truly compelling to know that adversities—traumas, problems, difficulties, ill health—can be managed differently. We can take greater control, we can empower ourselves, we can finally stand up and look adversity in the face and say, "Let's see if I can change this into a 'miracle'."

Look at what is transpiring in our society today. People are more empowered and more galvanized for action. Consider consumer groups. They are grabbing hold of critical issues and drawing the public's attention to them. They are shaping society. Political action groups, women's groups, minority groups, disabled groups, environmental groups—all these forces are shaping the way we live our lives. If these people can go ahead and empower themselves to make significant societal changes, we as individuals can empower ourselves to shape our own health and well-being. Unfortunately, we have been taught to give up our control. We have been brainwashed to turn our control over to various "experts" in our community. Certainly, sharing, networking, and asking others for support and help are important, but if we wish to tackle adversity, the first critical step is to gain control through the use of thinking, through the power of the mind. The rest will fall into place.

However, taking control is not so simple. We have learned to become experts of "the excuse." We have become comfortable in using our minds to generate reasons why we should not take charge, why we should not empower ourselves. We provide counterproductive explanations that can only foster helplessness, powerlessness, and grief. Rather than creating miracles, we produce misery.

OVERCOMING THE NEGATIVE INFLUENCE OF THE MIND

How many times have we heard people say, "I was born with this mess, and there's nothing I can do about it!" Eventually these people roll over and die, because they've given up—even before they've started. Why is it that two individuals with the same congenital defect resulting in paraplegia, for example, end up living distinctly different lives? Their outlooks are different, their thinking is different, their mindsets are different.

You see, the mind can be a tremendous ally if the reasoning that goes on inside is realistic, optimistic, balanced, patient, and flexible. However, the mind can be a devastating enemy if what goes on inside is opposite and contrary. The mind is a very powerful tool. If used properly, it can be a strong positive force.

Many people who experience relationship problems often use the "born with this mess" logic, quick to say that being born with "a certain personality" destines them to have relationship problems. Once you blame your difficulties on being born with a particular personality, you immediately erect an obstacle to change. This rigid and restrictive thinking blocks the prospect of constructive and worthwhile changes taking place. You have given up control of your life to your "inherent makeup." Congenital defects and specific personality traits will not prevent you from achieving greater well-being and happiness, but your mind and the thinking that goes on inside it can.

These days, parents seem to be society's convenient whipping posts for our woes and miseries. Now, our parents may have very well contributed to some of our difficulties, but to spend our lives assigning blame is useless. Rather, the crux of the issue is what are you now prepared to do about your problems? Are you now prepared to think differently so that you begin to take hold of your adversity and turn matters around? All of us find it easier, at times, to have a scapegoat—and our parents are ideal for that. But scapegoating removes the responsibility from our own shoulders, and with it goes a sense of control over our lives. Scapegoating takes the power from us and puts it into the hands of the person or persons being scapegoated. To overcome adversity, control must rest in our own hands. Don't give that control away to anyone else!

It's safe to say that basically we have been brainwashed into believing that there is always something deep-rooted in our histories that has caused our present problems. Some of us get trapped into thinking that unless this early turmoil is uncovered and understood, we will be incapable of maintaining a healthy and happy way of life.

Although early childhood traumas do occur—serious accidents, frightening encounters, sexual abuse, death of a loved one—they do not have to become insurmountable roadblocks. Because of the early influence of Sigmund Freud and others like him, we are all strapped with the unfounded belief that resolution of trauma is the only way to a peaceful and happy existence. There is absolutely no consistent or logical evidence to back this perspective up. Consider the millions of people who have experienced catastrophes in their early lives and yet are able to thrive and live fruitfully. They think differently, they keep their focus on the future. They refuse to let themselves be bogged down by past pain, failures, lost opportunities, or regrets. So remove the shackles of the past, discard those old clothes, and get on with it! The power of the mind is waiting to be unleashed.

Is old age really a deterrent? A lot of people seem to think so. No doubt health can fail, senses are not as acute, memory is not as reliable, and strength and endurance are not as dependable, but is succumbing to these challenges the answer? Many elderly persons have decided not to give up the fight. They have decided to show the strength of the "grey power" movement. These people have lobbied governments and politicians to ensure that their views, their issues, and their thoughts are well represented. They have achieved fantastic results. By droves, people in their 70s, 80s, and even 90s have proclaimed, "I refuse to lie down and wait to die." What a way to establish control. What a way to harness your energies and your drives to ensure a better life. What a remarkable outlook.

In our society we are most enthralled by our feelings. It is a common belief that our emotions are so powerful that they rule every aspect of our lives. How many times have you heard people say, "If I don't *feel* like doing it, I can't do it," or, "If I don't feel up to it, then there's no point in trying it," or even, "I feel rotten, therefore I look rotten." We believe that we are at the mercy of our emotions and therefore it follows that if our emotions are negative, our health, our happiness, and our lives will suffer. We are simply too controlled by our feelings and not sufficiently in control of our thinking.

No doubt feelings are important. They tell us how well we are doing or how poorly we are doing; how well we are fulfilling our ambitions, or not fulfilling our ambitions; how well we are managing our adversities, or not managing our adversities. However, feelings should not rule our lives. In fact, our "hearts" work in concert with our heads. More important, what we think determines how we feel rather than the other way around. If we begin to think in reasonable, flexible, tolerant, optimistic ways, we will probably feel more cheerful, more upbeat, more buoyant. Let us all expand our minds and begin to consider all sorts of interesting possibilities so that our hearts may flutter with joy and happiness as often as they can.

Our society constantly bombards us with very concordant messages. We are supposed to look good and feel good. We are supposed to be efficient, be successful, be youthful, be on the go, be attractive—feel good all of the time. And yet, people who demand to feel good all the time find themselves caught in a constant struggle against themselves. It is not realistic to be on "top of the world" all of the time. We run into a mess when we place such extraordinary pressures on ourselves. We spend so much time worrying about how good we are feeling or how poorly we are feeling that our problems multiply. To place unrealistic and illogical demands on ourselves defeats any attempt to make ourselves healthier and happier. To demand of yourself that you feel good all of the time may well contribute to your feeling bad a fair bit of the time.

Not only are there people who demand to feel good all of the time, but there are also people who seem to think that life never runs smoothly enough. Then we wonder why unhappiness and ill health have consumed our lives. After all, does life really ever run totally smoothly? Is not life like a rocky road with its bumps and curves? Rather than demand a smoothly paved road, let us prepare ourselves psychologically for the challenges ahead. Let us use our imaginations and the power of our minds to make the adjustments necessary to live the best lives we possibly can, no matter what the circumstances.

Self-confidence—the degree of trust and assurance that you can accomplish something, that you have the wherewithal to go forward and achieve what you set out to achieve. We place a great deal of importance on self-confidence. And it is significant that people typically feel more self-assured when they are more "successful" and less self-confident when they are "unsuccessful." In other words, we allow our actions to dictate how we feel and how we think. If we do rather well, then we end up thinking and feeling well. On the other hand, if we do poorly, then we end up thinking of ourselves negatively and feeling a lack of confidence. A marriage that does not go well, a debate at work not won, faltering health—we see these as signs of personal failure, which in turn justifies a lack of self-confidence. Furthermore, we reason that unless conditions change or unless we magically feel a surge of reassurance, there is no point in doing anything differently. This is the critical mistake. We wait for things to get better by themselves. We don't jump in and make them better! We stand back and hope for a miracle without committing ourselves to try and create a miracle.

Adversities that are not dealt with often become more severe. More important, the self-confidence to cope with them does not by itself appear and suddenly overwhelm us with its magnitude; it must be generated by our thinking. The view of ourselves that we create and the ideas we bring to life about our capabilities ultimately determine how we feel about ourselves and set the stage for our actions and behaviors. So grab hold of your mind and start to exert more influence over your life. Start to establish greater control over your difficulties.

We place a great deal of emphasis on others understanding our problems. Support and supportive relationships have become critical ingredients when it comes to dealing with adversity. But what underlies this is the misguided conviction that people have to appreciate what you are experiencing and what you are going through before you can get better. If they do not understand what you are going through, it will be a lot more difficult, maybe even impossible, for you to ever improve. This thinking can be quite damaging, especially when others do not or cannot appreciate what you are going through. How many people can truly and meaningfully sympathize with you? If others cannot comprehend the nature of your difficulties, it is not a catastrophe, but our dependence on their empathy could be.

We still hang onto the precious yet harmful idea that we have to be flawless. There are some who maintain that if we suffer a setback, we are surely flawed. What better way to guarantee continued unhappiness than to subscribe to this line of reasoning? People are by no means perfect. Relationships do not go perfectly smoothly. We are surrounded by flaws everywhere. We ourselves have a variety of "warts" both physical and emotional. Let us rejoice in our human imperfection.

Others should do unto you as you do unto them. If you are decent and respectful in your relationships with others, they should be decent and respectful in their dealings with you. Although fairness is a desired objective, it does not happen with great regularity. Often we are not treated as we treat others. People think, act, and communicate differently. We form relationships in various ways and yet many a relationship has faltered because of unrealistic demands that the exchange proceed in a specific direction of our own design. There are many unwritten rules, hidden agendas, and underlying expectations about fair play in relationships. No wonder almost 50 percent of marriages today end in divorce. We pressure ourselves and others unnecessarily, we create unrealistic demands of ourselves and others unnecessarily, and we manufacture adversities for ourselves and for others unnecessarily. Like most things in life, relationships can be worked out when reason, tolerance, flexibility, and acceptance prevail. Let us place our traditional rules and regulations in a big heavy-duty garbage bag and simply toss it aside. Managing things better involves some personal commitment to change. And as we have highlighted so far, that change largely involves a shift in thinking.

Bad things don't happen to good people—if only that were true. I'm sure many of us believe that we are good people, but unfortunately bad things still occur. However, some people have been brought up to believe that if we are nice, a bright light will always shine in our direction. We will not be burdened by the hardships of humankind. Because we subscribe to this line of reasoning, we end up feeling sorry for ourselves when a problem does arise.

Because we are all different, we handle things in different ways. Certain people manage their affairs more effectively than other people do. Some people are better able to handle adversities because they have developed superior problem-solving skills over the years. It is possible to acquire these problem-solving skills and that is partly what this book is about. However, because we are human, we have a tendency to compare ourselves with the next person, especially when it comes to handling life and its many puzzles. We often ask ourselves questions such as, "Am I as good as she is?" or "Can I be better than he is?" Not only do we compare ourselves, but we then proceed to judge and criticize ourselves for not measuring up. It seems as if we are always competing with the person next door, or vying with our colleagues, or rivalling other members of the family.

In essence, it doesn't really matter how other people are handling or not handling their difficulties. What matters most is what is going on in your mind. What matters most are the steps that you are prepared to take to make your situation better than it presently is.

When we are in the middle of a struggle, we often think that we're the only one in this mess. Because this difficulty is so unique, and our struggle is so great, this confusion will never get resolved. What I've discovered over the years is that there are very few problems that are, in fact, unique. The earth is inhabited by people in the midst of struggle, plights and problems that do not vary greatly from person to person. What does seem to be unique, however, is the internal turmoil that we personally create and experience. We may never have experienced certain feelings, thoughts, or sensations before. The pain, hurt, anger, and anxiety may never have been so intense or have lasted so long. But although the impact may be unique, the problem itself most likely is not. We truly are one of millions involved in any given struggle—struggle that can, with the right set of tools, be beaten!

The world truly would be a better place to live if people were nicer to one another, but to hope that your neighbor will be nice and that your problems will disappear is a hope mired in unrealistic expectations. People's upbringings differ, their personalities differ, their behaviors differ, their problem-solving abilities differ, and their degrees of "niceness" differ. Their unpredictable ways can make it very difficult if we expect only kindliness and humanness. Furthermore, we create more problems for ourselves when we overreact to others' failures to be compassionate and agreeable. We become angry, depressed, or anxious. So who is responsible for our problems? Is it all of those nasty individuals out there or are we in charge of our own destinies? The answer is that we are the main players. We are the chief stalwarts in our lives. If other people wish to behave obnoxiously, they can; if they choose to express themselves in an antagonistic fashion, they are entitled. We cannot be responsible for the behavior of others. However, we do not have to over-react and create more problems for ourselves. We *are* responsible for that choice.

"I'm sorry" is a phrase that many of us find ourselves saying over and over again. Those who are suffering from an illness or a broken relationship are often the worst offenders. We apologize for everything. We apologize for upsetting others, for putting others on the spot, for being too demanding—for even having problems at all. If we are struggling to make sense of our lives, to make sense of what is happening to us, why should we apologize? We shouldn't. However, there are those of us who are too senstive to others' reactions or to how others *might* react. We have to spend time thinking about why we have become so sensitive. We must rethink our position and take pride in the fact that we are trying to better ourselves. We are not going out of our way to try and hurt people. We're simply going out of our way to try and help ourselves. There is no reason to apologize for that.

Many of us are caught up with the question, "What if I don't get better?" If you try something new, if you dedicate yourself to changing the way you think and the way you manage your affairs, something is bound to happen. Breaking old patterns opens up new opportunities. More than likely you will feel better, you will handle your daily challenges more effectively, you will straighten out your relationships and your health and happiness will improve. That's what this book is really all about!

MAKING MIRACLES

People. Many people have helped me write this book. People from all walks of life. People of all ages. People who represent the broad spectrum of background and goals. What do these people have in common? The answer is the ability to confront—and conquer—adversity. And we are not talking minor setbacks, we're talking extreme misfortunes. What makes these people different? Read on. Their perspectives on life will intrigue you. Their views on their problems will fascinate you. Their ability to harness internal resources will impress you. You will find that they truly march to the sound of a different drummer. I refer to these people as miracle makers.

Excuses. You know the kind. Excuses not to change—even when change is the only hope for a better life. As you go through this book, make note of your own excuses. Consider how the people interviewed here have tossed aside their excuses and how their lives have improved as a result. After all, there is a choice to be made. We can hold onto old alibis or we can discard them and opt for a breakthrough. The interviews included here will convince you that you too have the strength, the tools, to choose the second alternative—that you too have the potential for making miracles.

THE INTERVIEW

To set the stage for the interviews that form the core of "*It Can't Happen to Me*," I developed a list of problems—some very serious, others less so —that plague humankind. From my many years in professional practice as a psychologist, and from revealing discussions with numerous colleagues, friends, and relatives, I was able to compose this list. The difficulties were divided into three main categories: (1) work, (2) marital/family/domestic, and (3) personal health/well-being/lifestyle. I then proceeded to construct an interview format, which is described in the next section. The interview questions focus particularly on the thinking process, from the onset of a given problem to its ultimate resolution.

After the problem list was established, and after the interview questions were devised, a number of health professionals were invited to participate in the project as interviewers. I first trained them to properly administer the interview questions. They were instructed to find and interview people who had overcome the 99 problems I described on the list, with no one individual being interviewed more than once. As a verification mechanism, I phoned, at random, a number of interviewees to confirm that the interview indeed had taken place and that proper procedures were followed. Permissions for the interviews were granted with the understanding that anonymity would be maintained.

The questioning clearly highlighted the prominence of thinking, a critical activity of the mind. Why? First, the influence of thinking upon health is a very significant interest of mine. Second, and more important, some of the most exciting scientific advances have been in such fields as Rational-Emotive Therapy, Cognitive-Behavior Therapy, Neuroendocrinology, and Psychoimmunology, all of which study the positive influence of the mind upon psychological and physical health. Therefore, I felt obliged to probe the cognitive domain to discover the inner beings of our so-called miracle makers.

It is my hope that you will gain some profound insights from this book that will positively influence your health, happiness, and well-being.

Sit back and enjoy this "miraculous" reading experience. See what you can learn. This should be a most exciting journey.

THE INTERVIEW FORMAT

1. Age:

2. Sex:

3. Occupation: Telephone Number:

4. Describe your adversity (i.e., problem/difficulty/trauma/crisis):
   A. What were the events that led up to it?
   B. What happened?
   C. How did it affect your personal life?
   D. How did it affect your life at home?
   E. How did it affect your relationships with family/friends?
   F. How did it affect your work?
   G. How did it affect your working relationships?

5. What did you think about (i.e., what went on in your head/what did you say to yourself) that kept your life in such a mess?

6. What new thinking went on in your head to help you challenge your old ways and overcome your adversity?

7. How did you then feel?

8. How did you handle the problem differently/how different was your life?

9. How have you been able to keep up this new outlook and this new way of living?

10. When you slip into your old ways of handling your problem, what do you say to yourself/what do you do?

11. What advice do you have for people who have the same problem?

When examining the interview questions, specifically items 5, 6, and 10, it could be argued that they are worded to extract exactly what I am attempting to demonstrate, namely, the importance of thinking in overcoming adversity. Therefore, it is necessary to explain the rationale behind these questions, and I will do so by offering these assumptions. First, people are always thinking but are not always aware of it because it is so automatic. Second, thinking does influence our entire lives but we are often not cognizant of how thinking negatively or positively affects us. Third, it is crucial to uncover these mental processes so that our thoughts truly come to the surface. This can be accomplished through direct and specific questioning that does not allow for simple "yes" or "no" answers, but require that the interviewee reflect upon and verbalize that which was previously taken for granted.

You will note that we have shortened the interview questions in an effort to let the interviewees' words stand on their own as much as possible. What were questions 4 through 11 in the actual interviews now read: Adversity, Self-Defeating Thinking, New Thinking, Emotional Response, Solution and Outcome, Sticking With It, Slipping Back, and Advice for Others.

PART 1

On the Job Front

1: JOB LOSS

Female, Age 28, Printer/Typesetter

ADVERSITY

Being newly graduated from school, I had no working experience and therefore was in no position to be fussy about which company I worked for. The first job that came up was for typesetting in a very small company. It was not what I had in mind, but just to gain experience, I accepted the offer for this rather low-paying job.

This company had only a small staff. I was the most inexperienced and the newest member and had to do all the duties around the office, even those that were not in my job description. These I undertook without complaint and just treated the situation as part of my experience in the working world. Benefits at this company were not good and the environment was not healthy because of very poor ventilation. I often had headaches. From my observations, the employer/employee relations were not good at all. The turnover rate of staff was high. Most stayed less than two years. Some stayed only a few months. I was to find out why. It seemed that this employer would give some kind of excuse to terminate employment when an employee was due for an increase in salary. Knowing this, I eventually planned to leave this company and look for another position. Two months short of my due date for an increase, I was handed a termination letter asking me not to return after my vacation. The employer had failed to give me two weeks' advance notice. What's more, he used my week's vacation as part of my notice. The reason he gave was that there was not enough work to maintain the existing staff and I was let go. Afterwards I found out that he had hired another person at minimum wage to take my place.

At first, I was in shock after receiving the letter and did not know what to do. I was very hurt and my ego was destroyed. All my life I was my parents' favorite child, an honor student, and a teacher's pet. I was always admired in school and at home. Now all of a sudden this person thought nothing of me. He did not appreciate me and terminated me! How would I face my family and friends? What if I could not find another job?

I ran home and locked myself in my room and cried and cried. Everyone at home was alarmed but dared not ask me what happened. When they found out, they told me not to worry and they were very supportive. But my ego was hurt! I lost a tremendous amount of confidence in thinking that I was not good enough.

3

My co-workers understood, but there was nothing they could do to comfort me.

SELF-DEFEATING THINKING

Why did this happen to me? I have always been highly regarded by family and friends. This person did not appreciate me! What have I done wrong? He was not fair to me! What can I do? My family and friends will think less of me and treat me as a failure! If I cannot find the same kind of work, what other job can I do? I do not have any skills. I am a failure!

NEW THINKING

Not everyone in this world has to like me. This employer has the right to treat me unfairly and even fire me if he wants. But it doesn't mean I have to sit back and take it. I am going to seek legal assistance about how I was treated. My family does not need my financial support and I do have their emotional support.

EMOTIONAL RESPONSE

I did not feel as lost as before, knowing that I had support from my family and friends and knowing that I was going to do something for myself. I realized that I had a lot of courage.

SOLUTION AND OUTCOME

I matured more from this experience. Even though I had the full support from my family and friends, I could not rely totally on them. I truly needed to rely on myself. I found another job soon after, with better benefits and salary. Also, my legal aide would be preparing a letter to be sent to my former employer about my termination.

STICKING WITH IT

I realized that I am in control of my life and although some rotten things can happen, I don't have to mope around and be depressed.

SLIPPING BACK

I often remember my experience and how well I handled it. I remind myself that I have courage and will fight for what I believe in.

Realize that you have a choice—to help yourself or not help yourself. Also, and this is very important, no matter how good you are, you might not always be liked and you could be fired for no good reason.

2: DEATH OF A CLOSE COLLEAGUE

Male, Age 47, Pipe Fitter

ADVERSITY

I was working in the machine shop at the time. There was some problem with the hydraulic doors and the maintenance department was asked to send someone to have a look at it and repair it. Two guys came, one of them was my friend. His buddy got called away to another area of the plant and my friend decided to have a look and try to fix it himself. He was up in this box attached to a forklift truck, like the box hydro services uses to change the street lamps, about 25 feet off the ground. I guess he was fiddling with the door mechanism, when all of a sudden I heard the sound of the hydraulic doors rising. I looked up and saw the door hit the box and knock him out. I could see him sailing through the air toward the far side of the truck. I didn't see him hit the floor but I heard it. I screamed out for help and started running toward him. He was lying on the concrete floor with this big gash in his head and there was lots of blood. Another friend arrived at about the same time and both of us held him down. Can you believe he was actually trying to get up. We stayed with him until the ambulance arrived, but there wasn't much that they could do. He died on the way to the hospital.

For weeks I couldn't sleep. I kept seeing him flying through the air and hearing him hit the ground. I was thinking about how he was trying to get up and I felt terrible because there was nothing I could do to help him. Consequently, I began to have headaches, so my doctor eventually gave me some pills to sleep. There were times I was nauseated remembering what had happened.

I drove my wife nuts! She's a light sleeper and before I was given the sleeping pills I was so restless, I'd keep her awake. For a while I was really paranoid, thinking of all the possibilities that could happen to any one of us. I was nervous about my son playing on the monkey bars at school or climbing trees; I kept thinking that if he fell he'd end up like my friend did. I was always yelling at him to get down from things. He didn't know what was happening inside my head and couldn't understand why I was so angry.

I didn't feel like socializing much; I just wasn't in the mood to see a lot of my friends. Whenever we did get together, somehow the conversation would get around to what had happened. All I wanted to do was forget so I avoided everyone.

For the first few days, I didn't even come to work. Just the thought of having to go back into the area made me ill. When I finally did come back, I avoided working in the area of the accident. I did actually go back to the site once and looked around the floor to see if there were still signs of the blood. Luckily there weren't, so I felt a little better. The headaches made it hard to concentrate on work, but luckily nobody said anything to me. Even now when I hear the hydraulic doors, my heart sometimes starts racing. I eventually transferred out of the department.

People can be gruesome. They kept asking me at work for the gory details and I thought they were all sick and couldn't stand to look at them.

There was one guy in particular who at the time of the accident just took one look at what happened and told everyone to go back to work, that there was a truck waiting to be loaded. He said not to waste time standing around because the ambulance guys and the nurse could handle things. To this day, I find it hard to be civil with him.

SELF-DEFEATING THINKING

I guess I was paranoid about dying or that something like that could happen to my family. I was angry at being so helpless. I hated that feeling. I just stood by and watched him bleed. I simply kept blaming myself over and over again for something that I might have overlooked that could have saved him.

NEW THINKING

I adopted a "live for today" attitude knowing that we have no control over how long we live. I finally came to accept that I did all that I could for my friend, and that the rest was up to fate and the unknown. Then I enrolled in a first-aid course. I know now that even if I were qualified at the scene of the accident, there wasn't much I could have done. The anger eventually went away when I realized this.

EMOTIONAL RESPONSE

I felt better; I felt more secure that I could cope with other similar situations having taken the first-aid course. It's great that I'm now accomplishing things in life and not procrastinating. I used to always put off doing things, saying I had lots of time—not anymore.

SOLUTION AND OUTCOME

I find that I spend more time with my family and I'm enjoying my kids. I used to work all the overtime I could, thinking that money was most important. I don't do that anymore. I try to live each day to the fullest. My kids are a lot older now and I don't find myself worrying as much about things that could happen to them. As a matter of fact, they took skiing lessons this winter and one son has started playing hockey. You know how rough hockey can be.

STICKING WITH IT

I truly live each day to the fullest. It's a lot easier than my old way of thinking. My wife has always held a similar outlook on life. She was always trying to get me to change my thinking. Now if I start slipping back to my old ways, she reminds me. My friend who was there at the time of the accident has been a lot of help. We have spent a lot of time talking about the accident. When I start worrying about things that could happen, he reminds me that I could end up spending too much time worrying and not enough time enjoying life.

ADVICE FOR OTHERS

Life is too short and sweet, so live it. If you are at the scene of the accident, just do whatever you can, anything could help. Time helps deal with the loss, and if you have a close friend you can talk to, this could help. I had my friend so I was lucky. We were both working through similar feelings. But remember, enjoy each and every day as if it was the last!

3: PAY INEQUITY

Female, Age 31, Greenhouse Supervisor

ADVERSITY

There were two of us in our department and we were the highest level technicians. Then one quit. When management tried to hire somebody for the position, they couldn't get anyone to take it for that amount of money. When they couldn't fill the position, they quickly increased the salary, making that position a level higher than mine. I went to my supervisor and we rewrote my job description, including new duties that I had taken on, in an attempt to get my classification reassessed. It went to the committee that does the evaluation for senior-level technicians. Their first inclination was to rate me even lower than I was currently and that made me really mad. They asked my supervisor to substantiate my revised job description, because they felt it may have been exaggerated. Fortunately my supervisor confirmed the description and supported my reassessment.

I was upset and depressed when I found out that I might get a demotion. And here I was expecting to get an increase just to remain on par with the other upgraded position.

I talked with my husband about it and we discussed different alternatives and options. Boy did I let off steam. They really had no right to do this to me. Many sleepless nights were spent mulling over the mess I was in and the way I was being treated.

At work, I wasn't throwing my heart and soul in it anymore. I did my work but when it came to doing extra, like work over Christmas, I declined.

SELF-DEFEATING THINKING

I was very angry. They had no right to treat me this way. My partner quit and they couldn't fill her job, so they wanted to hire a male and offer him several thousand more for the same job I was now doing. That was not fair. I simply couldn't stand unfair treatment and they shouldn't be allowed to get away with it, especially since the two jobs were originally classed the same. I thought about a lot of things, but mostly I was angry and frustrated.

NEW THINKING

The most important thing for me was to reduce the tremendous sense of anger, frustration, and hatred I was experiencing. I knew that if I allowed myself to go on like this it would hurt my health and I might eventually get fired from my job. I decided that they were entitled to do this if they wanted to, but they were going to have a fight on their hands. The minute I focused my attention on what I was going to do rather than what they should have done and how badly they treated me, I felt less angry and frustrated and more motivated to challenge them. I decided that if they were going to raise the other job, they would have to raise mine as well. In no way was I going to sit back and allow my job to be devalued while someone else was going to step into a reclassified job that was the same as mine, for more money.

I felt pleased and relieved at the same time, and I was motivated to proceed with my cause. Everyone knew my position, especially management. Management was not going to get off the hook on this one. My case was legitimate yet I would have to wait around three months until a decision was reached.

By the way, my position was upgraded and I received a comparable increase in pay. I was ecstatic! My efforts paid off.

EMOTIONAL RESPONSE

I guess I became more expressive and indicated how I felt and what I thought. I had not been worked up like this before. But it felt good because I did not let my anger run away with me. My case was presented in a logical and professional manner. I knew that my job was as valuable as the one they upgraded and I made certain that management knew it. After all, I'd been with the company for 10 good years and had made a valuable contribution.

STICKING WITH IT

I believe in myself and the work I do. Fortunately I also have colleagues who value my work and the contribution I have made.

SLIPPING BACK

I talk to myself and remind myself that my strong feelings don't have to get the better of me and don't have to get in the way of working through my problems. After all, it's hard to plan a strategy and be very angry at the same time.

ADVICE FOR OTHERS

Don't undervalue your position and don't undervalue yourself. You're important—even if others don't see it at times!

4: TAKING WORK HOME

Male, Age 43, Superintendent

ADVERSITY

It was a new job and the first time being the supervisor of six professional people. My problem was adjusting to this new position and proving myself worthy of this promotion. At the time, the company had stopped hiring, so there were real and perceived pressures to perform at the job. The company was also giving workers incentives to leave or retire because of cutbacks.

I had a computer at home, which made it real easy for me to take work home with me. Also, I had just bought a house, and this new job with a four percent pay increase would certainly help. There was pretty heavy competition for this position and I had to prove myself worthy of it.

Anyway, I began taking most of the mundane work home to do in the evenings, such as standard monthly budgets, standard monthly reports, and so on.

My personal life was unbalanced because I was spending too much time with work. Ultimately, this contributed to my divorce. I guess I wasn't in tune with what was going on around me. I assumed everything was fine.

As for my family relationships, well I just didn't maintain them as much. I lost touch with friends because I got into a routine of not going anywhere, except to work and back home to work.

This routine created a positive impression on the job. I was able to reach my objectives and take on more work. I probably made the group look more efficient by doing some of the work at home that I should have delegated. My workers had more time to spend on their projects and not be interrupted by the mundane chores that I was picking up.

My boss, those I supervised, and I maintained a positive working relationship. The boss was impressed because everything got done and that made him look good. The workers were happy because they were able to focus on project work, which they enjoyed, rather than be bothered by administrative duties. This scenario probably had a negative effect on my fellow supervisors because their managers would ask, "Why can he do all this and you can't?"

SELF-DEFEATING THINKING

I guess it's a drive to do your best as well as leave your mark. For me, achievement was the changes that occurred in the company because of my efforts. I wanted to feel that my being there made a difference, and that my hard work was paying off. It was a vicious circle; my hard work produced positive results, which prompted me to work even harder to get even better results. It all boiled down to the need for achievement at all costs. Because I was successful at work, it meant that I myself was important.

NEW THINKING

Seeing other people who, from my point of view, caused very little to happen in the company and yet received promotions. I started to ask, "Why the hell did he or she get that position when his or her work didn't seem to have much, if any, positive effect?" People who worked for me were getting promotions above my level, promotions that I had applied for. I realized that just because I think I'm successful, doesn't mean others think that way. Also, I shouldn't have been taking work home with me just to get "brownie points" and prove to the world that I'm great.

EMOTIONAL RESPONSE

I felt frustrated, annoyed, used. In some ways I felt stupid. I could have been spending my time doing other things outside of work and received the same recognition. I didn't even enjoy taking the work home with me!

SOLUTION AND OUTCOME

Well, I just stopped bringing work home. It didn't really have any effect on my job performance. During this time I got divorced, which triggered many unhappy memories about the quarrels I had with my wife over my strong commitment to work and not to the marriage.

Also, I basically stopped doing certain jobs because I felt they were useless. I repeatedly asked myself, "What am I doing this for anyway?" When questioned by others, I simply said, "The work will get done soon enough." I felt good about being straight for a change.

I started to manage my time better. I would go out at night for a drink with the boys, to a movie, or to dinner with close friends. I started bicycle riding and other physical fitness activities. Basically, I stopped doing what I thought I *had* to do.

STICKING WITH IT

I keep up this new way of living by deliberately leaving things at work. I manage my time better and don't spend time on unimportant matters. I learn to say "No! I just can't do it." I try to keep a balance between family and work. Spending time with my new wife and children is more important to me now.

SLIPPING BACK

I do occasionally slip back, and when this happens I remind myself that taking work home does not make me a better person or a better supervisor. I think about the old situation and ask, "Why am I working this hard?" I compare my work output with other people at the same level just to see if I am overdoing my share. I don't kill myself to do extra favors, but will do them on company time only.

ADVICE FOR OTHERS

My advice would be to discuss with your manager what is really important. Figure out the top three or four priorities and work on those. Put off or don't do the trivial items. Most of them usually disappear over time.

Thinking back, I would have questioned the importance of certain requests and would not have taken so much work home. I'd plan my day in advance. Remember, doing your best is fine, but overdoing it just to prove you're great can be a disaster especially if you find out you're not "great."

5: DISCRIMINATION ON THE JOB

Female, Age 36, Driver

ADVERSITY

I have been employed by the transit commission for eight years. When I was hired, there were 150 women employed and the remaining 4800 were male.

The ratio is now 500 to 5000. I felt almost from the beginning that the attitude toward women was patronizing. Then I made a minor error and the statement was made, "What do you expect, she is a woman." Another apparent problem was that my personal life and my relationships were blatantly slandered by the guys at work, and innuendos were made about what other female employees do after work. Occasionally, male customers refused to board my bus when they saw me, a woman, driving.

I had to be wary of dating male employees because of the gossip that would start up, although if a male employee was known to be after a female employee, that was fine and normal.

I have always been proud of my accomplishments and my independence. When I moved to the big city and took this job, I was pleased with how well I had adjusted. My father was also pleased with me and the fact that I had handled these changes so well. He was most supportive, and we often discussed my problems at work.

But these disparaging remarks were getting to me. I was angry and upset a great deal of the time, but fortunately I didn't show it on the job. Usually after work I would go home and often spill my guts to my father or a close girlfriend who was most understanding.

At the beginning, I was heavily involved with other workers socially because we had a lot in common and I thought it was important to be close with the people you work with. But then I discovered that a lot of drivers would be nice to my face but would gossip behind my back.

SELF-DEFEATING THINKING

I would often run home and scream "Why did this have to happen to me?" They had no right to treat me this way just because it was a woman doing a so-called man's job. I just didn't know how to handle it. Complaining would just make matters worse.

NEW THINKING

I thought about it constantly and talked to my father. Basically I came to the conclusion not to take it so seriously. I didn't have to let the subtle criticisms get to me.

EMOTIONAL RESPONSE

I felt like a burden had been taken off my shoulders. I felt like I had regained my self-respect. I knew that if I felt better, others might treat me better.

SOLUTION AND OUTCOME

I started to behave in a friendly manner, but more professionally as well. I gave up trying to be "one of the boys." Also, I began to express interest in my fellow employees, especially their spouses and children. All of a sudden, my working environment seemed to be friendlier, although I was careful not to be too friendly.

STICKING WITH IT

I remind myself of what I went through and the number I did on myself. Now I maintain a reasonable attitude; my expectations about how I should be treated are not unrealistic. I do the best job I can, I keep on schedule, and I am helpful to other drivers.

SLIPPING BACK

I do get frustrated and irritable at times but I recognize that it's normal under the circumstances. I'm careful to do things that won't damage my credibility that I have worked so hard to create. I reliably do my work and try to be helpful.

ADVICE FOR OTHERS

It's hard to change a workplace overnight. It's easier to change yourself. If you go out of your way to be as professional as you can be and at the same time keep your social life very private, things will probably work out. It's a shame certain people treat you the way they do, but it'll change, although it may take time!

6: WORK DEADLINES

Male, Age 29, Accountant

ADVERSITY

I just started a new job, which I took over from another accountant who resented management a great deal. She left the company two months before

I started. The job was temporarily taken over by someone who had a lot of other responsibilities that made it impossible to properly manage this position. A lot of work was left undone, disorganized, and in a mess.

When I arrived, work was piled up on my desk and every day more work kept piling up. I was faced with the dilemma of learning the policies and procedures, the routine of my job, as well as tackling a very heavy workload. In fact, I was carrying double the load of the other accountants in my group.

My wife and my two kids started complaining about my work, especially my working hours. I kept on staying late so that I could get the work done and meet the many deadlines. Even after my night courses, I went back to work and stayed there till midnight.

My whole life seemed concentrated on my job. Grocery shopping was strictly done by my wife, and cooking and housework were entirely her responsibility as well. I didn't sleep well, or eat well, and I began to lose weight. I didn't have any energy left for my kids, who even said that all I did was go to work. My whole world revolved around my job. We ate out a lot more and all I did was talk about my demands and my deadlines.

I didn't have time for friends and family. My friends thought that I had forgotten them so they never bothered to call me. I felt so isolated at times.

I tried to cope and get everything done, because I wanted to prove to myself that I could do it all if only I pushed harder. Initially I had all the energy, but later on I felt so weak and tired that I couldn't concentrate anymore.

Over time my patience with people decreased. I became more sensitive, and I resented people taking up my time.

SELF-DEFEATING THINKING

I thought that my workload was grossly unfair because I had double the load of the other accountants and I kept blaming my predecessor for the mess she had left for me. But in spite of everything I kept telling myself that I had to do it all.

NEW THINKING

I finally thought what good is it to complain about what my predecessor did or didn't do. I should start focusing on what I can do now. I also finally admitted to myself that I had limitations and I could only do so much!

EMOTIONAL RESPONSE

I began to feel less pressured and less preoccupied. I found that I wasn't as nervous or as edgy. I started to concentrate better and my patience with other people picked up.

SOLUTION AND OUTCOME

I looked at the overall picture of my work and started listing which items should be my priority. I talked to my boss and made him aware of my workload and informed him that no matter what I did I couldn't do it all. I met with all the people involved who were relying on my services and asked their opinion about what the essential priorities were. I made them all aware of my workload and my limitations as well. I also started thinking of my family, because what I was doing was not fair to my wife and my kids. My work is only part of my life, although an important part of it. Finally, I admitted to myself that I wanted someone to confide in and share my ideas with.

I guess recognizing my limitations and acknowledging that my job was only part of my life were major accomplishments. I also thought that although I was getting a lot of satisfaction from my job, it is not worth it if it hurts my health and my family. Things at home finally started to get back to normal.

STICKING WITH IT

I am now convinced that to have a good and enjoyable life there should be a balance of family, work, home, school, and friends.

SLIPPING BACK

I think about how miserable I had been before and I ask myself if I want to experience it again. I always get a "No" for an answer.

ADVICE FOR OTHERS

Accept your limitations, that is the key. Also, explain how you feel about the job, talk to your manager, there is nothing wrong in asking for help. The job is only a part of life, do not make it your total life!

7: BEING LAID OFF WORK

Male, Age 59, Auto Mechanic

ADVERSITY

The company where I had worked for almost 30 years was changing hands. The people who owned the building and the property had sold out because they wanted to give their son a car dealership. My co-workers and I were given the opportunity to remain with the new employer or seek employment elsewhere. I decided to stay. I hadn't worked anywhere else.

I thought I was getting along well with the other employees as well as with my new employer. As with most small businesses during this time, there were a lot of economic hardships and business was up and down. There had been two previous layoffs that amounted to a shorter work week for a temporary time period. Then came the third layoff notice—INDEFINITE.

We have always been a close family—wife, daughter, and three sons. I was content with my life as it was. My daughter and son-in-law were expecting their second child, one of our sons had gotten married the year before, and the twins from our oldest son were doing well in school. What more could a man ask for? My wife had not worked outside the home since our marriage. Now she was faced with going out to find employment to help with the finances.

I withdrew from my family and friends; I became depressed, started drinking, and turned into an angry person. I was informed that my new employer had no intention of retaining the previous employees, and one by one they left. My work record was pretty good and I felt he had no "just cause" for my indefinite lay off. When I investigated this further, I discovered that the owner had made accusations that I was untrustworthy. This made me very angry. I later filed a lawsuit countering this allegation on the basis that my previous employer had entrusted me with a great deal of responsibility and large sums of cash. I eventually won my case.

SELF-DEFEATING THINKING

I thought I was a failure; how was I going to provide for my family? This was my job—provider! I kept all my feelings inside, I didn't want to worry

17

my family any more than they were. My life was in a downward spin and there was no way up. The bills came in, groceries had to be bought, and I became more and more worried. More worry, more depression, more drinking, more depression, more worry. I was used by my employer. He used me for my knowledge of the building layout and contacts in the automotive business. Then he dumped me. I could barely be civil with my wife and family. My wife pleaded with me to get help, but I thought I was just fine. I was waiting for a miracle to happen. My wife went to my daughter and made her aware of the situation at home. My daughter gave me the "this is not the father I grew with" talk. I don't remember feeling so low as I did during this time in my life.

NEW THINKING

One day my daughter told me that if I didn't care about myself then they wouldn't care either. She told me that I was an important part of all their lives, but they were making themselves sick worrying about me. She made me take a look at myself and got me talking. Once I got started, she just sat and listened. When I was finished, I was ready to take a stand. I was able to see things in a clearer light. I was a good person and my life and my family were important to me. I was ready to take control. This was not the end of the world. The energy devoted to make myself miserable could be used to turn my life around. After all, I realized, being out of work doesn't mean that I'm a failure; it doesn't mean that I'm a rotten provider; it doesn't mean that I'm a bad parent or spouse. It simply means that I better find other work.

EMOTIONAL RESPONSE

I felt better about my situation, I was ready to get things together and I had motivation. I had a renewed respect for myself, and I enjoyed being with family and friends again. Waking up in the morning ready to face the day was an inspiring feeling.

SOLUTION AND OUTCOME

After being out of work for six months, I found employment that lasted almost a year. Due to economic difficulties I was laid off again. It wasn't quite so devastating this time. I really didn't like the job, although the people were nice. I didn't really enjoy being there, but I didn't feel that my life was falling apart. I think my family was more upset than I was. Within three days I found other work. I really enjoy this job. It is part-time, less responsibility, less pay, but I am content. We aren't wealthy, but I know we are not going to starve.

18

STICKING WITH IT

I take one day at a time. I find it easier to ask for help. I find that I am more willing to discuss my fears and concerns with my family. My wife now has a part-time job. I admit I am a little uncomfortable with the fact that she has to work, but I am learning to live with it. She feels that she is contributing to the household finances and I am learning to do housework. The nice part is that we seem to have a better relationship.

SLIPPING BACK

I take stock of the situation. I tell myself we will manage, we have survived before, we can do it again. I find that I don't get as depressed anymore. Anyhow, my children, no matter how busy they get, always have time to talk to Dad.

ADVICE FOR OTHERS

Think it through and use resources that you have. You are probably capable of more than you think. Don't be afraid to ask for help.

8: CHANGE IN JOBS WITHOUT PROPER SKILLS

Female, Age 42, Nurse

ADVERSITY

I accepted a job in a field I had no experience in whatsoever. I had worked in an operating room for many years and I felt it was time for a career change. I chose occupational health because it would mean working with healthy individuals and also it would mean working at a day job.

My employers realized I had no occupational health experience but my years in nursing had given me a varied background and I would learn on the job. I had a very short orientation period and my immediate supervisor was a perfectionist. She was intolerant of any mistake that was made no matter how insignificant or minor and did not see the need to repeat information if it had been given once.

I had difficulty coping with the expectations of my supervisor. Shortly after I started this job one full-time person was cut from our department. This left me in a situation where I not only had to learn all the skills and tasks for my new position, but I also had to take on the duties of the individual who had been let go. I had to take on too much responsibility in too short a time. I was under a great deal of pressure and stress each and every day.

I started to feel like I was losing my self-esteem and sense of self-worth. I began to question my own judgment and felt I couldn't do anything right. My spirit was being broken and I was loosing my personal motivation.

Frequently, when I arrived home from work, I would be in tears and would get down on myself. I was often spoken to in a very demeaning manner and I found it very humiliating. I also developed insomnia; at times I had difficulty sleeping two to three times a week depending on how bad my work situation was.

My family and friends were very supportive. They encouraged me to be more assertive with my supervisor and impressed upon me that I did not deserve to be humiliated and demeaned. I have had many satisfying jobs in my career and I should not let this situation cause such self-doubt.

After being in this job for approximately five months, I had lost total interest in it. I realized my heart was not in it and I can honestly say my performance did not live up to my own expectations. I was so obsessed with the way my supervisor treated me, I lost the motivation to learn and apply myself to the learning process. As a result, my skill development did not progress.

The relationship I had with my supervisor deteriorated to the point where we could hardly be civil with one another. My department has a part-time secretary. She and I became allies and gave each other the support we needed.

SELF-DEFEATING THINKING

I kept asking myself, "Why did I ever leave the operating room?" I had been so happy there and knew my job so well. I also had never encountered a situation where there was such a poor working relationship between myself and my immediate supervisor. I kept questioning myself and putting myself down. "What's the matter with you?" "You must be stupid." "You should try harder." "Why do you keep putting up with this abuse?" I began to believe that I did not have the ability to learn new information.

NEW THINKING

In my mind I knew I had to develop a method for getting my thinking back on track and not allow myself to be distracted. I began to recognize how obsessed I was with this supervisor and because of this obsession I wasn't able to concentrate on learning this new position well. How could I ever become skilled in occupational health if I was preoccupied with a supervisor who was a demanding perfectionist. I came to grips with some of my limitations as well. I was not assertive enough. I feared what might happen if I spoke up. Also, I realized that this was not the working environment for me. At first, it seemed like I was running away, but I told myself that I would work with this person for one year then I would seek new employment.

EMOTIONAL RESPONSE

Once I came to these conclusions, things changed for me. My job performance improved, I was more relaxed, and I was able to enjoy the employees whom I was there to help. I became more expressive with my supervisor and refused to put up with the emotional abuse that she was directing at me.

SOLUTION AND OUTCOME

I took an assertiveness training course and this helped me tremendously. I learned how to express my anger constructively. I developed techniques to help me in my stressful relationship with my supervisor, and was then also able to use these techniques to better help the employees at my plant.

I also learned not to get so wound up about my supervisor, a person who was like this with everyone.

STICKING WITH IT

I terminated my employment with this company and started job hunting. My self-motivation returned as did my self-confidence, and I landed a new job with a much better company. I knew I would manage this job change much better, because I would not allow things to deteriorate as they had in the other position. The previous year was most difficult, but I learned a lot about myself and others. Also, I now know that in order to learn new skills, I must try to create a reasonable working environment for myself.

SLIPPING BACK

I just remind myself that I have been through a very difficult year and now, thanks to my determination, I have turned my professional situation around. I keep telling myself if I'm willing to make things right, they will improve. I tell myself things can only get better if you make them that way, no one else can do it for you. If I'm going to learn something new, I must try to overcome obstacles as quickly as possible.

ADVICE FOR OTHERS

I would advise anyone else to speak with their supervisor much sooner than I did. Conflicts of a personal matter must be resolved before they reach the

21

point where it is too late to correct them and then your work suffers, especially if you're learning something new. I would also advise anyone with this problem not to let it beat them. Continue to do your best work and when you know you have done all you can to improve the situation and it still is the same, do as I did and seek new employment. I feel like a huge weight has been lifted off my shoulders and I am thankful for the opportunity to try again.

9: FIRING A CLOSE COLLEAGUE

Male, Age 52, Sales Manager

ADVERSITY

My problem was that I had to dismiss a person with whom I had worked for 12 years. In that time he had become a friend of the family.

He had a record of absenteeism, coming in late, and poor job performance. When I asked him if there was a problem he just shrugged his shoulders and said "No problem." I pleaded with him on several occasions to see someone about it and to make an effort to correct the situation, but he had no response.

One time I invited him and his family to my house for dinner. I got him alone and tried to explain the situation to him in a friendly, nonthreatening manner. Because of his ongoing absences and sloppy performance, his job was in jeopardy. He told me to mind my own business and walked with his family out the door. Three weeks after this one-way conversation, an employee was injured directly due to his negligence.

After trying unsuccessfully to get him to seek help, I knew I had to let him go. Because I was his immediate supervisor, I was the one to give him the bad news. It took me quite a while to do it. I guess I had to build up my nerve. One night I drank a few too many beers and had a fight with my wife, all because I was bothered by this whole affair. I actually tried to avoid the whole situation. If I ignored it, it would go away.

People in the office would ask occasionally what I was going to do with him. I would say that it would be handled as soon as possible.

SELF-DEFEATING THINKING

Well, for a while I noticed that he improved a bit. I thought that if I pleaded his case to my manager, I could keep him on. I guess I was avoiding my

responsibilities. His family, wife, and kids were friends of my family. I kept thinking that I was hurting the whole family. I believed that I would ruin his career. I had no right to hurt him and his family like this.

NEW THINKING

I came to grips with the fact that I had to do something. I just said to myself, "Look you're sticking your head in the sand." So I have to get on with it. I realized that it would not be easy, but that everyone does things that are difficult. I knew that it would be hard for me and hard for him, but if things remained the same, that would be worse.

EMOTIONAL RESPONSE

I didn't feel any better, in fact, I was uptight, nervous, and somewhat worried about what might happen. I just knew that I had to get on with it. If anything, I noticed that I was more determined than ever before.

SOLUTION AND OUTCOME

The day I asked him into the office he was late. I simply told him what the company's decision was. I gave no explanations, no excuses, and no apologies—although I wanted to say I was sorry. Our families haven't talked since. There was a lot of resentment, but I now know that it comes with the territory.

STICKING WITH IT

I actually haven't had to fire a colleague since that episode. If I had to do it again, I'd look at the whole thing in a more objective way. It's just a part of my job and not a very nice part, but what can you do. Also, I survived my nervousness, although I was hard to live with for a while.

SLIPPING BACK

When a problem comes up I guess I tell myself to get on with it, make a logical decision, say what you need to say, and get the hell out. I also recognized that it's often in the best interests of the employee and the company to get it over with, and get on with matters. No one benefits by allowing a bad situation to get worse.

ADVICE FOR OTHERS

I've learned not to mix business with pleasure. I don't know if that's a form of self-protection or not. I think I would advise other people in my position not to invite their work problems home. I would advise you that there are certain responsibilities that have to be met. If you have to fire someone, realize that it is not a personal issue. It is a decision done for legitimate reasons that in the end, it is hoped, will benefit both parties.

10: DELIVERING A POOR PRESENTATION

Female, Age 45, Health Care Professional/ Counsellor

ADVERSITY

I was asked by my manager to give a presentation to a group of supervisors and managers. Although I was knowledgeable in the area and knew my material, I was uncomfortable with this task because I had no previous experience in giving presentations to a large management group. I was only given two weeks to prepare for this. The presentation was delivered, but I was so nervous I rushed right through it. The feedback I received was that it was not a good presentation. I was mortified.

SELF-DEFEATING THINKING

I was angry and resentful that I had to do this in the first place, a task that my manager would have done had she not decided to take some time off. I did not bother to discuss my apprehension and resentment with my manager but instead stewed about it. I saw myself as a failure. I wished that I had excused myself from this task. Preoccupation with the idea of looking bad in front of others stayed with me for days afterwards. I thought I could never face my colleagues again because I was so embarrassed by the whole situation.

NEW THINKING

After many a headache and sleepless night, I woke up to the fact that at least I made the effort. There are others who would have run away from this experience, but I faced up to it and did it.

I know that I probably looked foolish, but maybe next time, and hopefully there would be a next time, I'd do a little better. After all, being good at delivering presentations doesn't come overnight. Sometimes I put too much pressure on myself by demanding instant success at whatever I do.

EMOTIONAL RESPONSE

I was relieved and seemed less intimidated by the possibility of giving another presentation. Also, I realized that we all get embarrassed once in a while and it goes away.

SOLUTION AND OUTCOME

I was compelled to improve my situation so I quickly enrolled in a program on public speaking and delivering effective presentations and seminars. I felt this would help me to handle speaking engagements more confidently.

STICKING WITH IT

I constantly remind myself of how I delivered my first talk and how I wanted to run out of the room and hide. It is only with continued practice and tough work that giving presentations will be easier.

SLIPPING BACK

I sometimes avoid public speaking opportunities, but usually I talk myself into doing them, then I go ahead and give the talk. What I also recall very vividly is the satisfaction and feeling of tremendous accomplishment after giving presentations.

ADVICE FOR OTHERS

It is critical that you take up the challenge even though it may be quite intimidating at first. I believe that it gets easier the more you take the time to be well prepared and the more you practice your speech.

It's also important to get some help or coaching by taking seminars on public speaking and delivering effective presentations. And finally, speaking to a group is a very threatening experience for most people and you should not be embarrassed about it, but if you do get embarrassed, it'll go away.

11: POOR WORKING CONDITIONS

Female, Age 31, Machinist

ADVERSITY

After 10 years at my job, I decided to leave. The shift work and working on weekends, let alone the physical and mental demands, finally got me down. I was always expected to produce more and more because our quotas got increased. More business was coming in and we had to keep up, otherwise we'd stop being competitive.

I felt very tense. If I slowed down at all, I was told and reminded about our targets. I think my children got so used to me not being there in the evening that they almost ignored me when I was there. My husband was supportive of whatever I wanted to do with respect to my job, but he must have been a little lonely at night too. We seemed to have little private time together. While on the job, I kept wondering how things were at home, which I guess is only natural with working mothers.

The funny thing is I really enjoyed my job. But the conditions—namely, those crazy hours—were doing me in.

SELF-DEFEATING THINKING

I was afraid to take the risk of quitting because I didn't really have any strong trade skills. I was worried about not finding other work, especially since we needed the money. Over and over again I kept kicking myself for not staying in school and getting a proper education. Then I might not have ended up in this rut. But I knew I had to make a decision, because I was becoming more stressed and I would bring it home with me and my husband and I would argue. But every time I was tempted to resign, I talked myself out of it by saying that it would get better sooner or later.

NEW THINKING

I realized that if I didn't risk leaving this job, then I might risk something else, namely, hurting the relationship with my husband and my children. How would you like to come home to your own kids who wonder whether you're living there anymore. I finally asked myself about my priorities in life and whether they were only work related. Surely my family meant something to me. One morning I woke up and said to myself, I'm going to do it!

EMOTIONAL RESPONSE

Relieved is the best way to put it. But I was also quite nervous, because I was finally going to do it.

SOLUTION AND OUTCOME

I went to my boss and, shaking all over, I said, "I quit." He was shocked. All my work friends were shocked as well. But as soon as I did it, I immediately said to myself that I had to find something else in a hurry. I remembered that another company had been interested in me a while back, but I hadn't taken it seriously at the time. So I went back there right away and, wouldn't you know, they wanted me and made me an offer on the spot. I thought about it and weighed the pros and cons because it was going to be for less money, although I would no longer have to work crazy hours. I decided that the time had come to do something for my family and also for myself.

Now I work Monday to Friday with my evenings and weekends off.

STICKING WITH IT

I try not to look back, although I realize that I enjoyed the work, my friends, and even the fast pace. But I needed a change. Now I have more time for my family, and every day I seem to be getting more relaxed.

SLIPPING BACK

I have no intention of slipping into my old pattern of working under crazy conditions, because it simply isn't worth it to me and my family.

ADVICE FOR OTHERS

Worrying about change causes too much indecision. A change can sometimes be as good as a rest. A well thought-out change, whether it turns out good or bad, is a learning experience. It sounds crazy but it's true. Also, if you don't think through what your priorities are, you may be confused for a long time.

12: CONFLICT WITH SUPERVISOR

Male, Age 42, Engineer

ADVERSITY

The project engineer I was working for was nearing retirement. He was being replaced by someone inexperienced in this field. Over the years, I had been pretty friendly with my boss, helped him on many a weekend with work on his home, and maintained a good social and working relationship with him.

The new guy was a younger man who became instant buddies with my boss who seemed to favor him almost immediately. My boss created an important project for this new man and more or less treated him with kid gloves. I got left some junk work that involved restructuring a project of very little significance and this made me as mad as hell. I felt like a lackey doing this useless project. Furthermore, this work had already been done before and I had my own projects to start on.

At home I was a terror. I fought with everybody. My wife and my kids would shy away from me when I walked in the door after work. I didn't feel like socializing anymore, because all I would do is complain about how poorly I was being treated.

One morning I decided that I had had enough of this insignificant work I was doing and went and blasted my boss. He was shocked because he'd never seen me behave this way. But I just couldn't put up with this situation anymore.

I told him that I was not going to participate in this restructuring project and that I was going to return to my other projects, which were more important. So I left his office and we remained in conflict for about a week.

I now became even worse at home. I never felt like eating supper—I just wanted to be left alone. One evening my wife came up and said that we had better talk. It was an interesting discussion because she made a lot of sense. When you're a hothead like myself, you sometimes lose your perspective, but she helped me to regain mine.

SELF-DEFEATING THINKING

I realized that I was very insulted. I had been so good to my boss and he was treating me unfairly. He had no right to dump meaningless work on my lap, I deserved better. After all, look what I had done for him, and yet he turned around and treated me like a lackey.

NEW THINKING

I never thought that my conclusions might be off base. I was second-guessing what was going on in my boss's head without really sitting down and talking with him about it. All I did was assume certain truths then went into his office and blasted him, and then I proceeded to maintain the conflict. What an eye-opener. I'd never really questioned my perspective before but it made sense to do so now.

EMOTIONAL RESPONSE

I felt kind of foolish and silly. I probably should have spoken to my boss directly rather than spend a week ignoring him.

SOLUTION AND OUTCOME

I went in one working day to my boss's office, closed his door, and we had a heart-to-heart talk. I was straight with him about how I felt insulted and overlooked. I thought that I was being moved aside in favor of this new individual. What my boss then said surprised me. He first stated that I was very important to his group and that the restructuring project was an essential first step in a much larger project, which I could potentially head up. The work that had been given to the newer employee was designed to ease him into his new position. When I left the office, I felt like an idiot for behaving like a child, but I also felt relieved that I was not being pushed aside.

STICKING WITH IT

I now realize how unnecessary all that aggravation was. Here I was getting all hot and bothered, upsetting my wife and kids, and for what? I was just too premature in my judgment of this situation and as a result I alienated others and upset myself.

SLIPPING BACK

I say to myself think, think, think, before you act, you might save yourself and others a lot of grief.

It is always better to first think it through, then confront the conflict straight away and get it resolved, before people become entrenched in their positions.

13: LACK OF COMMUNICATION ON THE JOB

Male, Age 23, University Student

ADVERSITY _____

As a university co-op student I had to have a job for a work term. The most interesting jobs required more qualifications than I had as a junior student. The job I finally took was with a health club as a fitness instructor. My boss was really looking for someone with business experience as well. The club was in some financial difficulty and desperately needed more members.

As soon as I completed the school term, I was to show up for an orientation. He discussed what he wanted me to do and then on the second day, I was given a list of tasks and then he disappeared for the day.

He regularly disappeared but always had time to criticize all of my work, including such efforts as posters for advertising. He would not tell me what he didn't like about anything—he would say, "do it again." I became very emotional about everything. I was constantly dejected because no matter what I did, it was not enough—no positive feedback, only criticism. He just didn't know how to communicate with me or for that matter with anyone else.

I was irritable with my mother and father, even the cat! I complained constantly to friends and family about how terrible work was, how horrible this boss was, and how I could not wait for the work term to end. School would be great in comparison. It reached the stage of, "Screw you, you're not teaching me anything; you're not even paying me the agreed salary." I kept doing extra hours of work and I felt royally jerked around.

It got to the point where I would try to avoid him as much as possible. I have the theory that you never burn bridges so I felt avoidance was the best tactic with my boss (that way I couldn't tell him how terrible I thought he was). But I was still upset. And people kept telling me that I had changed. I wasn't as much fun to be with anymore because I was obsessed with this boss who didn't know how to talk decently to me.

SELF-DEFEATING THINKING

This can't be happening to me. How am I ever going to get through this period. I couldn't see myself lasting another four months. My mother told me to make an appointment with my boss and tell him exactly what I felt and offer him suggestions about how we could communicate to improve the working relationship. This made good sense, but I wasn't sure that it would work and he might criticize me even more.

NEW THINKING

If this is to be a learning experience, I must get the most out of it. No matter how uptight I feel, I better sit down and talk with him otherwise he will never know what's on my mind. I'll tell you, I had many sleepless nights worrying about this one.

EMOTIONAL RESPONSE

I felt edgy, nervous and jumpy. My parents noticed that I couldn't sit still and they always tried to comfort me.

SOLUTION AND OUTCOME

I sat down one morning with my boss. My knees were shaking. My voice was even cracking, but I told him that I thought that we were having a communication problem and that I wanted to work it out.

He said, "Fine," and asked me what I had in mind. What we worked out was a schedule. Once a week, we were to get together and discuss what was accomplished. He was to tell me what I had done that he liked and also what improvements I needed to make. The strange thing is that this schedule only lasted a week. After that he would disappear before our scheduled meeting. But the most important thing was that he left me alone. I became more cheerful and humorous and found that I was serving the clients better. We simply had no further run-ins. In fact, he was complimentary on occasion.

STICKING WITH IT

I remind myself of how unhappy I was until I sat down with my boss. The communication problems really did not improve that much, but it didn't

31

matter. What was most important was that I did something about it, even though I was scared shitless.

SLIPPING BACK

The easy way out does not get the best results; the hard way out does get the best results.

ADVICE FOR OTHERS

Tell your boss what you're thinking and feeling no matter how difficult it is. Even if your boss still doesn't listen to you, at least you've tried to make it better!

14: DEALING WITH ANGRY CUSTOMERS

Female, Age 52, Supervisor—Credit Collection

ADVERSITY

My job was directly in conflict with my nature, as I am a helpful sort of person. I had to call people when they were late in making payments to get them to pay their bills. I had to be stern while advising them the terms of payment and then give them deadlines. Their accounts would be cancelled if they failed to pay up. Once they offered an excuse or got very angry and upset with me, I would either back down and say, "Okay, you can pay later," or be frightened by the customers' show of anger and then terminate the conversation. Or, I would go to the other extreme and get angry in return and make all sorts of threats and accusations.

I would often take my work home with me, but only to tell my family about some of the irate customers with whom I had to deal. On the other hand, I would sometimes blow up at colleagues. One time I got so upset with a customer that I slammed the phone down and then blasted someone I worked with. It was so upsetting to me that I came home crying. I just didn't seem to be handling these customers well. I needed to find a balance between being angry and being too soft, otherwise I wasn't so sure that I would be able to last at this position. When you start to take out your bad moods on the people you work with, then it's time to take a serious look at yourself and decide whether you are suited for this line of work. How could I be more confident and take greater control of the conversation?

SELF-DEFEATING THINKING

I said to myself that I just don't fit in this job. I either get too involved in their sob stories or I get so troubled by a bitchy customer that I immediately threaten to cut off their account. I thought that I would never amount to an effective credit supervisor.

NEW THINKING

I read something about staying focused; that is, to stick to the message that you are delivering and not get sidetracked by other details such as a sob story or a customer's angry temper. I realized that I wasn't calling people to upset them, or to hurt them, or to shame them, or to embarrass them. I was simply pointing out that they needed to get their credit account in order otherwise their credit might be suspended or even cancelled. I reasoned that I was trying to motivate the customers to get their finances in order. After all, I'm not a hurtful person, although some of the customers I spoke to really got hurt. This is when I truly needed to stay focused and remind myself of the purpose of the call.

EMOTIONAL RESPONSE

I felt in control. For the first time I felt more confident in what I was doing and why I was doing it. That didn't mean that everything would be perfect from now on. I simply felt more certain that I could get my message across without blowing my cool.

SOLUTION AND OUTCOME

I began to manage my conversations better. I said what I had to say and the minute I found myself drifting away from the original message, I corrected myself. Now the customers still didn't react any differently, but I did and I felt good about it.

STICKING WITH IT

It's not easy especially when some irate customers really tell you off, but I remind myself that I did not put them in a mess, they put themselves in that mess. I'm only trying to tell them to get their credit in order. Also, when they're annoyed, it's not really at me but at my message, which is a reminder of the mess they're in.

SLIPPING BACK

I tell myself, "Don't lose your cool, stick to the point and stay focused!"

ADVICE FOR OTHERS

There are angry people everywhere, not only customers, but it doesn't mean you have to resort to anger to deal with them. You can present your message clearly and logically. But also don't think that because you're in control that you're going to be treated any differently. People may still choose to chew you out, but you don't have to upset yourself in reaction to them.

15: OFFICE POLITICS

Female, Age 41, Administrative Assistant

ADVERSITY

The problem was that I simply wasn't kissing my boss's ass. I'm sorry for being so blunt. Because I didn't make him feel like he walked on water, he didn't acknowledge many of the suggestions that I offered and those that were acknowledged were put down. Eventually, I was passed by for a promotion to which I was clearly entitled, all because I didn't play the game. It came to the point where I could hardly look at him, let alone communicate with him. What he really wanted was for me to agree with everything he said and did, and then praise him for being such a wonderful leader. But most of his ideas really didn't make sense, and he was always getting in trouble with his manager because he didn't know what he was talking about.

At home I was frustrated, short-tempered, fatigued, less productive, and simply not pulling my weight. I talked to many a friend about this mess and all they kept saying was to ignore it. I even took sick time just to escape my boss. Ordinarily I never would have done this.

I was confused at work. I thought my ideas for improving the office were worthless because of the criticism I was receiving. Also, I kept disagreeing with my boss's plans, which weren't sensible, and yet I had to follow his rules. I could feel my enthusiasm slipping. I began to withdraw and not contribute. My co-workers even covered for me so that my boss wouldn't see that I was slacking off.

SELF-DEFEATING THINKING

I thought I was a failure. I was defeated; my self-esteem was in the pits. I believed that I was no longer making a contribution. Any idea I had was discounted or criticized and rejected.

NEW THINKING

There comes a point in time when you finally realize that you have to get out of your mess. I recognized that I was the only one who could really deal with it. There really wasn't too much that I could do with my boss because he treated me like he treated everyone else. He was always threatened by suggestions whether they came from me or from others. He could not face the fact that his ways were not the only ways.

I began to remind myself of how successful I'd been as a student, as a mother, as a volunteer, as a professional in other companies for which I'd worked. Once these ideas ran through my head, the confusion cleared up and I was ready to start planning my strategy.

EMOTIONAL RESPONSE

I was greatly relieved and felt all of a sudden that I had more freedom of choice and more power over my own career. I could use this newfound energy to my advantage; I no longer had to feel defeated.

SOLUTION AND OUTCOME

I calmly assessed my situation and figured out what I needed to do to make it better for me. There was no point in hoping that my boss would change because he never would. Instead I decided to take a transfer, which was a step down on my career ladder. Although it was seen as a demotion, I would still have the same responsibilities, I could plan my own work, I could be creative with ideas for improving the office, and, most important, I would no longer report to my boss. His criticisms would be history.

STICKING WITH IT

I remind myself of how productive I am now, how much more creative I am, and how much more of a contribution I am making to my unit. Also, I am so much more comfortable with myself and my working environment.

SLIPPING BACK

"Stop this shit" is what I shout at myself. I step back and remind myself of how far I have come along. Then I ask myself what I just did to get into this rut. Am I overreacting to someone's impression of me? Once I clear my head, I think of my options and plan a course of action.

ADVICE FOR OTHERS

Be your own person. Don't conform to a mold. Don't overreact to situations. Learn from criticism and grow to be a better professional.

16: EXTENSIVE TRAVEL FOR WORK

Male, Age 42, Salesperson

ADVERSITY

My job involved being on the road a lot. I was lonely when I was away from my children, wife, and home life. Eventually my wife became so bored she committed adultery. Our relationship became increasingly distant. I wasn't involved in family life. I wasn't involved in any school-type activities with my children.

I lost friends because I wasn't around to enjoy any social activities. Contact with them was virtually nonexistent and they kept wondering why I never had time for them.

My anxiety started to become overwhelming. I felt I didn't have anyone to talk to. My attention span decreased and I couldn't concentrate at times. It was as if my world outside of work was crumbling around me.

I didn't feel I could communicate well with my peers, who were somewhat short-tempered with me because I was always complaining. So who was there to share my thoughts with? No one. No one at home and no one at work.

SELF-DEFEATING THINKING

I had to be successful at work. My one salvation was to be the best salesman and make the most money. Success and material wealth were critical. I was convinced that if I worked hard and provided for the family they would realize why I was doing this. I figured they would understand that I had to be away. As my family life fell apart, I worked even harder, thinking everything would pull together on it's own. In the end it didn't of course.

NEW THINKING

I finally came to the conclusion that the more I was away, the more family problems escalated. I had become obsessed with work and success. Not that there is anything wrong with success and wealth, but it consumed my life to the exclusion of everything else, especially my deteriorating home life. So I decided that I would continue to strive for success but not at all costs. I finally came to the conclusion that I wanted more from life than just material wealth.

EMOTIONAL RESPONSE

I was ecstatic that I had made this decision. I felt really happy inside and couldn't wait to share it with the world. I now hoped and figured that I could pull my family back together. The funny thing is, now that I was so excited about this change in myself, my wife still wanted all the extra money that she had grown accustomed to.

SOLUTION AND OUTCOME

I took another job at a different location as a branch manager. This resulted in more regular hours and substantially reduced travel. I now worked a standard nine to five day, Monday to Friday. Even with the work changes and less travel, I didn't notice any improvement in my marriage. After about one year, I accepted a job as a branch manager at another location. However, my relationship with my wife never improved. I guess that it had passed the point of no return. Finally the relationship became so strained that we separated. After we separated things did not return to normal. Eventually, we got a divorce and went our separate ways. What a price to pay for success.

STICKING WITH IT

At first, I didn't handle single life too well. I had always had a family. I tried to make myself happy with a renewed social life to take up time, which now wasn't spent on travel or a family.

I eventually bought a home in another city and continued as a salesman, this time selling a different product line altogether. I spent a lot of time with my two children. I was disgusted with my ex-wife, because I had worked so hard and my vision of a family had been torn apart. But I have grown to accept this new reality and trust that I can reestablish a meaningful personal life.

SLIPPING BACK

Well, I just do not travel anymore. I have remarried and I've made a new life for myself. I am still basically a salesman, but I don't travel overnight and do most of my business within the city. I talk a lot with my new spouse and we have very good open communication. I certainly know when my wife has a problem. I have learned to listen; however, it took me a long time to learn.

I have come to realize that anything done in excess has a price attached to it. During my first marriage I travelled far too often and that among other things contributed to the failure of the relationship. Never again will I repeat the same mistake.

ADVICE FOR OTHERS

Don't ever assume anything, communicate everything. If you have to travel, phone home and occasionally take the whole family with you. You have to confront and solve your own problems. You can't sweep your problems under the carpet and hope they will disappear.

If I had my life to do over, I wouldn't have let problems drag on so long, and maybe my life would have turned out differently. Looking back, this stressful lifestyle could have ended three or four years earlier before my first wife became so disillusioned and started having an affair.

17: LACK OF RECOGNITION FOR WORK

Male, Age 25, Produce Supervisor

ADVERSITY

I was having problems with my managers and my co-workers concerning my job performance. Due to conflicts with my co-workers, I was not being recognized for the good work that I had done.

I had been working for a grocery store for about 10 months. Assigned as a produce supervisor, I got to know the store routine very well and was often asked to help out in other areas such as grocery, dairy, deli, cash, or office. This pleased my general manager, but my good performance was resented by my immediate boss and other fellow employees. To them, this only meant that the general manager would expect that same quality of work from them. They showed their resentment with false accusations, and even went so far as to mess up boxes and groceries that I had stocked after completing my shifts. They complained to the general manager and because he didn't want any more problems, I was suspended without pay. Nothing was done to rectify the situation, and my ten months of good service was never acknowledged. I eventually got my job back but things were not the same; I found it even more difficult to work there.

During this time, my personal life was affected. I was not the same with my girlfriend. At home there was considerable friction, as I often argued with my parents over the matter. They were not very supportive—my parents said there wasn't much I could do, whereas I wanted to change the situation. Also, I noticed that my health was affected because I started to get violent headaches and stomach upsets, neither of which I had really experienced before.

SELF-DEFEATING THINKING

After this incident, my attitude in the workplace changed. I only did the duties that were expected of me, and didn't offer to do anything extra than what was required. I punched in and out on time instead of staying past my shift to finish a job. I suppose I resented my boss and my co-workers for doing this to me, and, as a result, I was more spiteful than before. I was very angry at them. I believed that when a company hires you to do a job, and you do it well, you should be rewarded and not punished. I wanted a raise, not a suspension. I focused on negative thoughts of revenge, maybe going to a lawyer to solve the problem. Also, I interacted as little as possible with my co-workers because I no longer trusted them.

NEW THINKING

After all was said and done, I realized that this resentment was only making matters worse and I knew that this would not improve the situation. I didn't want to quit my job, so I just returned to work and continued with my job as if nothing had happened. I blocked out negative thinking and replaced it with reasonable thoughts of getting a job done well, not to please someone else, but for my own satisfaction. This was the driving force behind everything I now did.

EMOTIONAL RESPONSE

I felt better about the situation and working there wasn't so bad anymore. I just kept doing my job as if nothing had happened, and the other workers left me alone after that. I didn't care what others thought of my achievements—after all, I felt that I was doing it more for myself this time. I also knew I was handling things well, and this new attitude made a difference. I was no longer worried about making a good impression with my managers, and I learned to enjoy my job.

SOLUTION AND OUTCOME

I made sure that management was kept informed of what was going on in produce. I made a checklist as to what I had accomplished during my shifts. This way, I had documented proof on what I had done and there would be no discrepancies. I felt that I shouldn't run away from the problem, but rather that I should handle it in a positive way. My life was better after this because eventually my managers gave me the praise and credit that was due to me for my good service to the company. My relationships with my co-workers improved; but those who still resented me, I left alone, and they left me alone. It didn't matter to me what my co-workers thought, but when they complimented me for a job well done, I felt good about it.

STICKING WITH IT

I thought back on my past experience and I realized that I was concentrating so much on getting praise from my managers and co-workers that I neglected to praise myself. I realize now that although it feels good to be complimented or recognized, I shouldn't expect or demand to be recognized for all my efforts. Just because they don't praise me for my work, doesn't mean my work performance is any less worthy. I have been able to keep up this new way of living, and there is less stress in my life because of it. I no longer feel that I always have to satisfy certain standards, and there is no need to prove my worth to anyone.

SLIPPING BACK

First of all, I tell myself that there will be times that I will feel unrecognized for good service. Instead of going to the manager and demanding recognition or a raise, I accept the fact that things will not always go the way I'd like them to. I accept the fact that many times my efforts will go unnoticed, yet I continue about my work as best I can. I know that eventually praise does come, and if it doesn't, then it doesn't. I also remember that sometimes it is better to change one's attitude and outlook than try and change the whole workplace. Certainly, it has worked better for me.

ADVICE FOR OTHERS

My advice is to focus on your good qualities and efforts, instead of waiting for or expecting praise from someone else. Accept the fact that things will not always go the way you'd like them to, and people may not always see the good things that you do. Accept this reality and don't strive to be perfect in the eyes of other people. This outlook will benefit you in the long run.

18: STUCK IN A TRAFFIC JAM

Female, Age 29, Stockbroker

ADVERSITY

The snow was coming down, the weather was miserable, but I had to make this meeting. It was an important deal that had to be closed at 10:00 A.M. As I hopped into the car, I heard on the radio that there were a lot of traffic accidents and cars were not moving. But I was going on the highway and was convinced traffic would be moving. Sure enough I was on the highway no more than a couple of miles and there it was, the biggest pileup I'd ever seen. And the cars were not moving. I was now stuck in a terrible traffic jam.

SELF-DEFEATING THINKING

I kept thinking it's late, it's late, it's late. I was panicky like never before. I screamed out loud that I needed this deal and that I would lose it if I didn't show for the meeting. I swore, I yelled, I pounded the dashboard. All of a sudden I thought I was going to black out.

NEW THINKING

Was I trying to give myself a heart attack? Was I that crazy? How important could any deal be if it threatened my health. I told myself that if I lost the deal it was not the end of the world. Hopefully, they would appreciate that the weather was bad and that I was trapped in a car jam. I'd never been late for an appointment, this was the first time.

EMOTIONAL RESPONSE

I immediately calmed down. My heart stopped racing, my breathing slowed down, and I stopped feeling like I was going to pass out.

SOLUTION AND OUTCOME

The minute I settled myself down, a great solution came to me. I pulled the car onto the highway shoulder and used an emergency phone booth. I eventually contacted my business associates and another meeting was scheduled. Then I went back into the car and listened to some relaxing music.

STICKING WITH IT

I now realize that certain things can't always be controlled. When you try to change something that can't be changed, you may end up hurting your health. I actually thought that I was going to black out in the car because I got so wound up.

SLIPPING BACK

I simply tell myself that I'm in the middle of a jam that I can't get out of, so why kill myself over it. There is nothing that cannot wait.

ADVICE FOR OTHERS

Stay calm and stop by a phone booth if possible so that the people who are expecting you won't worry.

The first thing to do is talk yourself down by reminding yourself that there are very few things that cannot be delayed for a later time. Next, settle yourself down by possibly putting on some relaxing music. Finally, realize that you might be able to come up with a solution to your dilemma if you remain worry free. Remember, I was able to think of using the phone on the shoulder of the highway only once I was able to calm down!

19: POOR PERFORMANCE REVIEW

Male, Age 52, Marketing Director

ADVERSITY

Fifteen years ago I came to this city and set up a sales and marketing company in North America for the parent company that was then based in Europe. Six years ago the parent company was sold off. My organization and another subsidiary company separately bid for the rights to own the North American sales and marketing operations. The subsidiary company won the bid and control of the North American company. I decided to stay on despite the fact that their man took over my job and was instated as my boss. This person and I simply did not get along. We differed in our approaches, and he tried to force his methods down my throat. But I resisted and this led to a major problem. When he called me into his office to give me a performance review, I was ready for the worst and it certainly came. I walked out of the office shaken, because never in the history of my career had I received such a negative review.

SELF-DEFEATING THINKING

What right did he have to judge me so harshly just because we didn't see eye to eye? For the first time, I really felt like beating up on someone. That someone was this asshole. I was furious. My track record was outstanding, yet he chose to overlook that and made the claim that I was not moving in a direction consistent with the company's new "strategic vision." I guess I really took his comments to heart but only for a brief time.

NEW THINKING

My new boss gave me a poor performance review, but I realized that no matter how hard I worked to correct it, it would probably not make any difference. In his mind I would always do a bad job. Although it was tough to convince myself, deep down I knew that he could come to any conclusions that he wanted to. After all, if he wanted to believe that I wasn't performing well so be it. However, the results were different. I was bringing in great contracts, my clients found me to be very responsive, and objectively I was doing well. This is what I repeated to myself over and over. Also, I believed that he was not too astute nor did he have good "business smarts." Whether I had respect for him or not, I decided that I would have to learn to work with him and if I continued to do things well and continued to have good results, maybe he would eventually change his attitude about me.

EMOTIONAL RESPONSE

My fury and anger faded away. Also my self-respect resurfaced. I have pride in my work and I still wanted to do the best job that I could. The people with whom I had worked over the past 10 years were very supportive, as was my family.

I continued to believe in my own abilities, but still felt my boss was an asshole.

SOLUTION AND OUTCOME

I committed myself to hanging in there and doing my work well. More and more, I was convinced that his perceptions of my performance were unjustified, however, since I was committed to staying in the company, I developed an interesting way of dealing with him. I simply ignored him and when I did need to speak with him it was brief and to the point.

STICKING WITH IT

I was able to maintain this approach because it worked. I did my thing independent of my boss and got the results. On the other hand, he kept away from me and walked around believing that he was managing this organization well. So we both got what we wanted.

SLIPPING BACK

I remind myself of what I have accomplished and the positive goals that have been reached as a result of my abilities.

ADVICE FOR OTHERS

Take a close look at your abilities and talents—and refuse to let your boss destroy your self-confidence. But if your boss does severely criticize you and give you a poor appraisal, it does not mean you have lost your abilities and talents. They will always be with you, even if you find that they have to be displayed in another company.

20: SERIOUS INJURY ON THE JOB

Female, Age 31, Press Operator

ADVERSITY

I was doing overtime in a factory on a punch-press machine. There was no guard mechanism on the machine and I reported it. Unfortunately, I was instructed to go ahead and finish what I was doing without the guard, as I only had a few items left to finish.

I put my hand down into the machine and must have accidently activated the pedal with my foot causing the punch to come directly down on the middle right finger. This finger was crushed in the press. I had eight operations to try to restore the hand so that it functioned well again. I continued to have pain and the surgical repairs did not fully restore the use of my hand.

I felt very depressed and frustrated. My right hand was so bad that I had great difficulty with grooming and personal hygiene. My self-image was the pits.

At this time I also had a newborn baby and being right-handed made caring for my child very difficult. Although I got a great deal of help from my husband, this did not eliminate my feelings of frustration, and at times I showed my impatience with both my husband and the baby. I had to go for physiotherapy every day and found it very awkward as I had to use public transit and bring the baby with me for my daily hospital visits.

My impatience was increasing to the point where one time while caring for my baby, I thought that I was going to literally crack up.

My husband began blaming himself for letting me go to work after the baby was born. If I would have stayed home, none of this might have happened. So I had to contend with my feelings as well as his guilt. He tried to help me with the housework and the baby as much as he could, but he was working shifts and this made it very difficult.

Obviously I could not return to my job at the factory, so I thought about other possible work. But I didn't know what to go after, because my right hand wasn't properly healed and I wasn't able to do what I really wanted to do. I wanted to work as a hairdresser or as a dental assistant.

So you see I was constantly frustrated and agitated because the "right job fit" didn't seem to be there for me.

SELF-DEFEATING THINKING

Why me, why me, why me! I couldn't tolerate the agony of not working. I blamed the doctors for not treating me well so that I could return to work. I thought that I would never get out of this mess. It would just go on and on, and no one including me, would know what to do.

NEW THINKING

One day I asked myself, "How can people with a terminal illness cope?" I'm alive and in good health, and I have a supportive family. The only thing out of order is this right hand, which hopefully will heal properly. If it doesn't, I will live with it and do the best I can.

EMOTIONAL RESPONSE

I was so excited and renewed that I couldn't sit still. Here I was going beyond my handicap and taking charge of my life. My outlook and my self-esteem turned right around. I was ready to face the world again.

SOLUTION AND OUTCOME

It took me a while, but I found a job as a health records clerk in a doctor's office. I finally was doing a job that I could physically handle, in spite of the fact that I was still experiencing pain in my hand. I took control of my life rather than leaving it to professionals, none of whom could agree on the type of care I should get. Few of them related well to me, and it was time that I looked after my own future.

STICKING WITH IT

Since I now enjoy my job, my focus is no longer on the discomfort in my hand but on accomplishing a full day's work and making my day much more satisfying. My injury is no longer so important to me.

SLIPPING BACK

I'm convinced in my own mind that sooner or later it will get better. Also, I am careful to rest my hand regularly. I have also stopped complaining and my close friends can verify that. If I start again, I tell myself to shut up.

ADVICE FOR OTHERS

Don't harp on the pain. Realize that although the pain sometimes comes back, there are certain things that will help relieve it. Learn to ask advice from the caregivers while recovering so that you know exactly what jobs you should be steering toward and steering away from. Know your limitations. Insist on good communication linkages between all the specialists who are treating you so that you don't get confused by opposite points of view. Most important, keep repeating to yourself, "It's going to get better, it's going to get better." Then get involved with living life.

21: BALANCING WORK AND HOME

Female, Age 31, Ambulance Driver and Attendant

ADVERSITY

My husband was a workaholic—always out of town and working long hours. His answer for being gone all the time was that he was providing me with all of the material things I'd ever need, hoping that this would pacify me.

We grew further and further apart and both of us took on other interests. He eventually moved out leaving me with two children, one 2 years old and the other 3 months.

I felt very stressed out. I had a lot of responsibility placed on me, having to raise two children with no job.

Eventually, I had to sell the house and find other accommodations for the three of us. I also had to get a lawyer to ensure that I would get proper support from my now estranged husband.

My relationship with my family changed dramatically. I had been very close to my mother, but when she found out that my husband and I were separated, she became very upset and somewhat distant. She felt that there was no reason in the world that could ever have justified such a drastic move. However, my friends were great and very supportive.

SELF-DEFEATING THINKING

I thought that I would never be able to support my two children. I was trained in secretarial work, but how much money would that bring in? I kept telling myself that it would never be enough to pay the rent and put food on the table. I constantly feared for the safety and security of my children. Every night I'd go to bed saying to myself that we'd never make it! I wanted to work but then what about my kids? I was driving myself crazy.

NEW THINKING

One time a close friend said to me, "The worst fear is fear itself." I was paralyzing myself with constant fear and worry and at the same time getting nothing done. So I said to myself, "The hell with this panic, do what you have to do to get your life in order." I knew that I'd be struggling for a while, but who wouldn't be under the same circumstances.

EMOTIONAL RESPONSE

I felt scared and under pressure to succeed. But I was also excited at the prospect of taking charge of my life and getting on with it.

SOLUTION AND OUTCOME

Immediately I got a job as a secretary and also enrolled in school to be trained as an ambulance driver/attendant. I'd always wanted to help people and this was an exciting career opportunity. There was a fabulous woman down the street who took kids for the day. Fortunately, she was able to look after both of my children for a reasonable charge. Things were now tight financially, which meant that I had to organize my priorities very carefully.

STICKING WITH IT

I'm very ambitious and have a tendency to drive myself to the limit but this is the only way to get ahead. So I push on knowing that I will provide better for my children and establish an interesting career for myself.

Since my divorce from my husband, I have become an ambulance driver/attendant. I am still concerned that my children are properly looked after, but both are carefully cared for by the woman down the street who has become a close friend. My oldest child may soon be enrolled in a special morning program at school. As far as my career is concerned, the more I achieve the better I feel. I'm thinking of pursuing a program to become a paramedic.

SLIPPING BACK

The minute panic and worry enter my mind, I simply remind myself of what I've accomplished and what I still plan to accomplish. But also, I think all of us are prone to a bit of worry and panic when we take risks in life. When I think about it, I've come a long way over the last number of years and its important to reflect on that once in a while.

ADVICE FOR OTHERS

Believe in yourself!

22: FEAR OF RETIREMENT

Female, Age 71, Retired Receptionist

ADVERSITY

I was raised during the war. At age 19, I was taken to work in a munitions factory. The war went on, and at the end of it, I married and stopped work till my family moved to Canada from overseas. Then for 25 years, I worked in the automotive industry as a receptionist for a car company. For me it was a prestigious position. Even though it was a receptionist position, it was important to the company and an integral part of the organization. I greeted and then grew to know many people. A few years before retirement, an efficiency expert came in and decided that this position for our company was a thing of the past. My job was eliminated.

At that point, I had about three years to retirement and would lose considerable pension if I left. The company didn't force me to retire but instead provided me with only one option, to work at the switchboard. I hated this a great deal, but the thought of retiring was worse because I had built my identity and my social life around work.

My husband and I have been together some 46 years, but throughout our relationship we have done many separate things. He was content to stay home, read, walk, and so forth, whereas I felt that being as active as possible was best. I threw myself into work, I enjoyed my friends, and I established a very active social life.

As retirement approached, I grew more uneasy and distant from those around me. My husband—a gentle, understanding man—always wanted to retire, so he couldn't understand my feelings or fears. I realize now that I was a difficult person to be with, but I felt like I was being put out to pasture. I didn't want a retirement party, those things were only for "has been." I may have been approaching 65 years old, but I had always prided myself on looking younger and having a young attitude towards life. I had too many things left to experience. I had this vision of retirees sitting around having tea with fellow retirees and discussing the good old times. I wanted to keep living the times! I suppose my husband as well as my family and friends humored me by saying retirement would be fine. These were going to be the golden years. Company policy stated that I couldn't stay anyway, so I had to get used to it. Most people look forward to stopping work, whereas I was just getting started. I wanted to take courses, learn about the computer, improve my typing so I could get off the switchboard and into something else. At times, the management at work became my enemy. They were forcing me out. First, they got rid of the reception area, now they were getting rid of me. Friends and colleagues at work couldn't and wouldn't talk to me about my upcoming retirement.

SELF-DEFEATING THINKING

I truly believed that my life was coming to a close, not because of ill health, but because I would no longer be working. I enjoyed having a routine in my life. I enjoyed going to work, being productive and useful. My friends were at work, yet because I was the oldest person of the group, I would be the first to go. I thought my life would come to a stop without work. My husband did very little all day and I would simply become like him, doing nothing, with nothing to look forward to. I was too active, too vital to just sit with people my own age, have tea and reflect on memories. Retirement was like a death threat to me.

NEW THINKING

Until my formal retirement, I thought this way. I did have a party. I graciously attended and hated every moment of it. But I was brought up to have manners, so I put on the act of a lifetime. I'll never forget the first morning of retirement. I woke up early as always, ready to go to work. I got dressed, ate breakfast, and went out the door. However, I caught myself before driving away and went back in the house. I cried much of that day, but my husband couldn't understand my feelings because he loved retirement. I went on this way for a few weeks. Then a friend of mine sat me down one day and told me I was wallowing in self-pity and would have to make retirement what I wanted it to be. All of my friends at work were still my friends, only I would have to make an effort to meet them for lunch or in the evening, not at work as before. Also, I had been a long-time member of a women's club. My girlfriend suggested I become more active in the club. Retirement would be what I made it. My husband had done this; he wasn't lazy or bored, he was doing exactly what he wanted to do. Relaxation after 60 years of work was perfect for him. If busy was what I still wanted, I needed to take my energies and redirect them. This really made sense. I'd never been a quitter, why was I doing it now? So I decided that I would live the life that I wanted to live.

EMOTIONAL RESPONSE

I felt like a new person. Retirement had now become a challenge for me. Just because I wasn't leaving for work each morning didn't mean I would have to stop enjoying myself. I felt so much better. Retirement meant only a reduced income, but my husband and I were financially comfortable, so the reduction did not pose a problem.

SOLUTION AND OUTCOME

My life took on a different direction because I became very involved in the women's club. I became President for two years. In addition, I returned to a great love—sewing. I began to sew for friends and family. In fact I began to see my family more often, where previously I was too caught up in work to spend a lot of time with them. Because I was able to change my attitude and thinking towards retirement, I stayed active. I'm more active now than when I was working. My life didn't really end with retirement, it just took off in a new direction.

STICKING WITH IT

I suppose I have kept this new outlook because I have made my retirement what I wanted—an active, involved extension of my working career. I'm sure in some people's eyes I have never retired. I guess I haven't, but there is no commandment on what retirement has to be. It can be filled with travel, relaxation, and new challenges such as taking courses. Retirement can be as exciting a phase in life as any other phase.

SLIPPING BACK

This doesn't really apply because I'm so busy. I sometimes think that I should give up a little of what I do, but I won't do that. I have spent most of my life being involved, and even at 71, I'm not willing to miss out on anything. My husband still reads, walks, and relaxes. And me, I'm spending a lot of time running around and taking advantage of my opportunities. I realize I'm

51

trying to live as much of life before I'm not able, yet I've been fortunate to be blessed with good health, so I'm able to do many things.

ADVICE FOR OTHERS

Do what you want. Even if you think others will laugh or ridicule you—so what. You only have one life and it's as good as you make it. Plan your retirement before it happens. We all know it will eventually come, so decide ahead of time what you want to do with it. Try to develop other interests besides work, so that leaving your job isn't so traumatic. Broaden your life at every opportunity, so that retirement just becomes an extension of life and living.

23: REENTERING WORK AFTER A PROLONGED ABSENCE

Female, Age 47, Student

ADVERSITY

My marriage had dissolved and I was faced with raising my 12-year-old on my own. Naturally there were many financial concerns and I was forced to return to work. For most of my married life I only worked part-time as a skating instructor and that was mainly for fun. Therefore, I had to make some major decisions about what I was going to do with the rest of my life. The main problem in returning to work was that I wasn't trained to do anything. I married young and my husband had always supported me. Unable to find a suitable job, the other option was to return to school—that was a big problem.

At age 45 I decided to return to school full-time and fulfil my career ambitions. It took two years and they were the roughest two years of my life. Never did I believe school work would be like this.

It affected my personal life in that it felt like a social shutdown. My family always came first, but school was second, and friends came third. Friendships were put on a temporary hold, whereas some of them were strong enough friendships to last through two years of absence. Other friendships were lost and in fact there were a few very serious arguments with people who did not accept my explanation that school was full-time work. Time spent with my children suffered and this troubled me more than anything.

It was such a change in lifestyle. I couldn't afford to travel; shopping sprees were out; I was using public transportation to get to school after having a car for years.

I was able to get part-time work just to bring in some extra money. However, there were times when I couldn't make it into work and then I'd get hassled by my co-workers who told me that I was not contributing and wasn't making an effort to be part of the team. This kind of feedback just shattered me because they didn't understand what I was going through.

SELF-DEFEATING THINKING

I was in school with a much younger group of people and I really didn't belong. It was a very isolating experience. I was really down. How was I going to cope through two years of it? Why was I doing this? I just wanted an easy way out, namely to run away. I said to myself that people who didn't understand my predicament had no right to criticize me for not living up to their expectations.

NEW THINKING

I was obsessed with reaching my goal and once I focused on that and adjusted to my new lifestyle, I forced myself to think through my problems. Once I graduated and had my diploma, my life would be different. I would be doing what I always wanted. This constant reminder kept me motivated and self-directed and I realized that there would be no turning back from school until I was finished. Now if certain friends and my co-workers couldn't understand what I was up against, so be it. These people did not have to be part of my life. In the past I never would have believed this. But now was different. I alone had to make it and nothing would stand in my way. A slogan would always come to mind—"When the going gets tough, I get going."

EMOTIONAL RESPONSE

Once I realized that there would be a light at the end of the tunnel and I knew I was coping, I felt reenergized. I also began to accept my ups and downs as being a normal part of this whole process.

SOLUTION AND OUTCOME

I simply plugged along, reminding myself constantly of my goals. Although I didn't have the money I was accustomed to during married life and had no time for socializing, it didn't matter anymore. I simply dealt with things one day at a time. Also I began to dress differently so that I would fit in more easily at school, and it seemed to work. I really forgot how old I was and just lived the life of a student.

STICKING WITH IT

This experience has made me a very disciplined person. I have become so goal-directed that nothing will stand in the way of my completing that diploma program. Because of this determination, I have felt stronger psychologically and at times I feel that I could almost tackle anything.

SLIPPING BACK

When in a rut, which really doesn't happen that often, I sit down and talk to those who are closest to me and who are prepared to listen and understand. Also, I take some time out by going for a walk or by going to a movie. But deep down, I am clearly aware of my one goal—finish the program and graduate.

ADVICE FOR OTHERS

Set realistic short- and long-term goals. Think about what you might like to do and then get lots of information on it. Make an informed decision to do it and then stick to it.

Being a student today is very different—everything is self-directed and you are more or less on your own. If possible, try to work when in school because it is another indication that you are in control and can take charge of your life. Finally, seek support from those who are willing to support you.

24: HARASSMENT

Male, Age 33, Male Attendant

ADVERSITY

I was working on a medical floor and one of the patients was diagnosed with AIDS. I'll call him John. John and I were getting along just fine. While I was on my coffee break, he had paged the nursing station because he wanted his food heated in the microwave. The nurses at the front desk told him that he was in isolation and wasn't allowed to use the microwave after his food was brought into his room. The nurses told me what had happened. He then paged again and asked for me. When I went into his room he asked me if I would heat his food up in the microwave. I explained to John about the isolation regulations. He then became defensive and shouted at me and screamed that I was no good, that I was prejudiced against him, and that I shouldn't be working in this field.

I took what he said about me personally, I couldn't help it. He then proceeded not to talk to me. I also heard that he was bad mouthing me to other staff and even to his relatives.

I never discussed this with my wife because I didn't think she'd understand.

As the days went on, I made a point of avoiding him. I wouldn't even look in his room, but I knew I was running away from my problem.

SELF-DEFEATING THINKING

I thought that I just could not face up to his criticism of me. It had ruined my confidence and I was simply taking the whole matter very personally. Out of control was an apt way of describing my predicament. I simply didn't want to go to work for fear of running into him.

NEW THINKING

I started realizing that the situation was affecting not only my work but my personal life. So I then decided to talk to other professional staff about the problem. People were very supportive. They told me that my work can be very emotionally draining and I'd have to learn not to take things personally. They emphasized the importance of separating my work from my life at home. This may be obvious, but it struck me that John was extremely angry about having AIDS and that he was probably displacing his strong negative feelings onto me. It was this insight while talking with my co-workers that really hit home.

EMOTIONAL RESPONSE

I started feeling more optimistic and actually ventured in to see John again. He attempted to intimidate me and kept making crude remarks under his breath. I concentrated on being professional and doing my job to the best of my ability. I reminded myself of the fact that the rest of the patients appreciated what I was doing for them.

SOLUTION AND OUTCOME

I didn't take negative comments that patients said about me personally. Since that one incident I've been verbally harassed by other patients, but I've kept

55

reminding myself that if I'm doing my job to the best of my ability, it's all I can do.

STICKING WITH IT

I'm working in a different area of the hospital now. I see a lot of different types of patients from all walks of life. Whenever someone verbally harasses me, I put it in perspective and don't take it personally. Most important, I usually don't take my job home. I'm very fortunate that I have mastered that skill.

SLIPPING BACK

I try to keep it in perspective and tell myself that unfortunately, it goes with my profession. I realize that I have to be a little more understanding with patients because they are ill and are apt to take it out on somebody else, namely me. I try to put myself in the shoes of someone who is seriously ill and has to spend a lot of time in the hospital. This must be very difficult for them to deal with.

ADVICE FOR OTHERS

It is very hard not to get upset after someone verbally harasses you on the job. I guess the only advice I can give is that you have to look at it objectively. People can and will be abusive when you least expect it, and there is not too much you can do to prevent it. If you are unable to deal with it, go out of your way to develop a different perspective so you don't drive yourself crazy. And most important, don't bring your job home with you, because your time at home is for you to enjoy with family and friends.

25: LACK OF CAREER OPPORTUNITIES

Male, Age 49, Regional Franchise Manager

ADVERSITY

After 20 years of service with the same company, my job was deemed obsolete. I was simply told that there was little available for me in the new organization. There was a corporate reorganization whereby the company was bought out by a competitor.

I was offered a change in position or a severance package because of my length of service with the company. I took the severance package because the management position they offered me did not fulfil my career expectations. The offering was basically a dead-end opportunity.

I became extremely mistrusting and cynical. Talk about stress, I was a living example. The sense of uncertainty was overwhelming. Here I was uncertain about a new job and uncertain about the future. Embarrassment was overwhelming, because I'd never been out of work. Now I was unemployed and very much ashamed of it. It was hard for me to keep my head up.

SELF-DEFEATING THINKING

Why did this happen to me after all I did for the company. Those bastards simply screwed me! By not offering me any real opportunity, they simply forced me out. My mind was filled with revenge.

NEW THINKING

I've always known that I'm good and I guess I had to remind myself. Also, I heard it from friends, colleagues, and relatives. It's funny how you can forget to believe in yourself. I was determined to prove to myself that I could get what I wanted.

EMOTIONAL RESPONSE

Ready for the challenge. Have you ever had sleepless nights because you're so geared up and ready to go? Well that's how I felt. I was so keen that I was bubbling inside.

SOLUTION AND OUTCOME

I went out and quickly secured a fabulous job as manager of marketing operations for a medium-sized company. It finally hit home how marketable I really was. I didn't really appreciate this fact until I was forced to look for work.

STICKING WITH IT

By acknowledging in our present working environment that loyalty is not what it used to be 15 years ago. Today, one has to constantly look out for one's own best interests.

SLIPPING BACK

I constantly bring myself back to the realization that no one is secure in their job. So I am prepared for the worst should it ever happen again.

ADVICE FOR OTHERS

When there are no worthwhile career opportunities available for you and you choose to leave with a severance offering, do not regard it as a poor reflection on you and your self-worth. Go out and aggressively market yourself and get on with finding what you want.

26: JOB DISSATISFACTION

Male, Age 36, Senior Business Analyst

ADVERSITY

I hated my job at the bank. I felt unfulfilled, disinterested, lethargic, and unrewarded. The office politics drove me crazy and I found I could not engage in the team approach that this particular job demanded of me. The disinterest I felt at work spilled over into my family life and I was lethargic and miserable at home. I became unproductive and uncaring. I thought if I was fired from my job that would be fine with me.

My friends and family remained very supportive because they saw I was unhappy and tense, but my attitude was, "Who gives a shit"!

SELF-DEFEATING THINKING

I thought of things like: "It's not my fault, it's their god damn fault." "Why should I work on a project I didn't believe in." "I don't believe enough in our goals to work at it." "I hate this mess I'm in."

NEW THINKING

With a great deal of support and consideration from family and friends, I came to accept myself. I recognized that I'm not a team player, rather I like to do things my own way. I did a great deal of soul-searching to come to these conclusions. I came to realize that it's hard to buck an established corporate system that has a set of values that are inconsistent with your own. In essence, I rejected this environment and acknowledged that I would never conform to these norms.

EMOTIONAL RESPONSE

Scared shitless. I was nervous about what might lie ahead, but I was also high about finally understanding who I was and what I needed to do. I also came to the realization that what I had been preaching to others, I had finally done myself. Don't let society and money overpower your personal search for happiness or satisfaction.

SOLUTION AND OUTCOME

I quit my company and started my own business. My life changed considerably. I relaxed more, the corporate work pressures were gone, but money was still a concern especially if the business ever failed. I knew then I would have myself to blame. There was a bit of tension at home, because even though my wife supported my decision, if there was any suggestion I wasn't doing my part at home, she would be certain to let me know about it.

STICKING WITH IT

My new outlook is I play the game, but by my rules. I satisfy my goals first. I recognize my employees' needs, but I'm also aware of my personal needs and the needs of my family—and both of these are satisfied first. I am now easier to live with.

SLIPPING BACK

I do things my way. The pressure I felt as a prisoner in the corporate world is gone. It is replaced with a sense of accomplishment and achievement. My family recognizes it and so do I. I'm still not easy to live with at times, but I find it easier to apologize. It's great to believe in yourself more.

ADVICE FOR OTHERS

Do what you believe in regardless of economic impact and personal frustration, but be able to accept the consequences.

27: WORK OVERLOAD

Female, Age 46, Payroll Manager

ADVERSITY

During the past 15 years with the company, I had always been placed in difficult areas that needed to be brought up to standard. A company decision was made to centralize all payroll operations. I was then promoted to Regional Manager, covering a large territory. My workload increased threefold. My number of staff tripled. Each operation in my territory had unique systems and procedures, and all of them had to be integrated within a four-month period, which took it's toll on all concerned.

One payroll operation was completely shut down and then relocated to the largest city in my region. Once the operation was reestablished, there was no support staff there to ensure that proper systems and procedures were in place. So new staff had to be recruited and trained, which in itself became a burden because there were constant demands to create proper payroll banking standards. While I was being pulled in 20 different directions, staff turnover mounted because there was too much pressure and stress. Problems with payroll banking and payroll processing intensified because they were being handled by inexperienced human resource staff.

In the middle of all this, my travelling increased. I had to travel frequently all over my region to train human resource staff. Long working hours were the norm both at the office and at home in order to keep on top of this increased workload.

My personal life was a mess because of the stress. I was exhausted and unable to relax.

My home life was affected because there was not enough time to do some of the things I enjoyed doing, as I was constantly tired. My relationships with family and friends were affected because I did not have time to communicate with them.

My work was affected because I did not have enough time to cover all bases as thoroughly as I would have liked.

These pressures were simply turning my world upside down. I was on a merry-go-round going nowhere.

SELF-DEFEATING THINKING

I believed that I was obligated to honor my commitment to this new position at whatever the cost. This is what kept me in a bloody mess. I did not want to walk away from this thinking I was a failure.

NEW THINKING

It took a lot of soul-searching but I decided that I needed more out of life than working seven days a week. I wanted to enjoy the simple pleasures. I have only one life to live and it was going down the tubes rather quickly. "Who needs this?" was a common expression of frustration that I finally took to heart.

EMOTIONAL RESPONSE

I felt numb and disappointed, yet I knew my decision would be the right one.

SOLUTION AND OUTCOME

I realized that the more I accomplished, the more would then be added to my overloaded basket. The merry-go-round had to stop. I walked into my boss's office and resigned. No longer would I worry about the workload, the pressures, and the people.

STICKING WITH IT

By staying away from overload situations and by accepting the fact that I no longer wanted or needed a career. I moved to a small community where the cost of living was quite reasonable. I rented a small house by the water and worked on my crafts. Actually, I've been making sufficient money from the sale of these crafts to cover my living expenses.

SLIPPING BACK

I reflect on past experiences, meditate, and live one day at a time!

ADVICE FOR OTHERS

Tone down your drive to succeed, because if you have a proven track record you are always called upon to solve problems that, over a period of time, can be very stressful and may in the end affect your physical and mental well-being. Learn to relax. Do not be fanatical about getting things done. There is always tomorrow.

28: DEMOTION

Male, Age 37, Electrician

ADVERSITY

Our economy was slowing down and interest rates were high at that time. I worked at an auto parts plant that was notorious for cost-cutting measures. Because I had the lowest seniority, I was told one morning that I would be laid off unless I was prepared to take a demotion. I had no idea how long the layoff would be so I decided to take a significant demotion. I lost close to fifteen thousand dollars in salary.

I had four kids, a wife, and a big mortgage to pay. My wife worked full time but I was always bringing in the most money and almost everything and everyone depended on me. All my children were still going to school. But suddenly, we had financial problems.

We always spent more than we had and kept saying that we should put away some money for a rainy day. The rainy day was here, but there was no extra money lying around. Suddenly we had to budget our funds and this for us was a strange exercise. The children, who wanted more and more, were restricted in their spending habits, yet they couldn't really appreciate what had happened to us financially.

We're not close to my brother or my sisters, so we knew we couldn't depend on them to help us. We had friends, but we couldn't go out and ask them to assist us financially. We had too much pride for that.

SELF-DEFEATING THINKING

I kept asking myself, "What am I going to do? Why the hell was I demoted?" Although I knew that I was low man on the seniority totem pole, I still found it hard to accept. I started to worry about missing mortgage payments and being kicked out of our house. Where would we then go? Life seemed so much easier for us in the Philippines. I had a secure job with good pay and benefits, and my wife also had a good job. But we couldn't go back home.

It wouldn't be fair to the children. They had a better chance of living a good life here.

NEW THINKING

Well, I said to myself, "I am a skilled professional, have gone to University, and have a degree in electrical engineering. There is a job out there for me." Luckily, at the time, there were a lot of opportunities available for someone with engineering skills. I realized that if I stayed with this company, I would have many regrets.

EMOTIONAL RESPONSE

I was motivated and keen to get going. It felt like there was a light at the end of the tunnel.

SOLUTION AND OUTCOME

I went out looking for another position and found a good job with great benefits in just a few weeks. I ended up doing the same things I did in the previous job. I was thankful that my parents supported me while I went to University and got my degree. I was happy with my new job and met a lot of interesting people. It was easier now to walk around with a more positive attitude.

STICKING WITH IT

While working full time at this new job, I got invited back to my old job. This new job was more demanding than I had anticipated. Putting in 16-hour-days was the norm for the last few months and I was getting physically and mentally exhausted and didn't spend much time with my family. In having to choose between the two positions, I decided to return to my old place of employment.

SLIPPING BACK

Shortly after I joined, the auto industry began slowing down again and there was talk about recession and a slow down in our plant. Most of the employees in our plant had been there a lot longer than I, so there was always a chance of me being laid off. Again, the signs of instability and insecurity were staring me in the face.

I tried to keep a positive attitude. I hoped that I would find a job if I did get laid off, but I didn't worry about it every minute.

My eldest child had been working as a nurse, my other two children were finishing college this year, and my youngest was in seventh grade. All my kids were still living with us and they helped out financially. However, if I was out of work, I honestly believed we would manage.

ADVICE FOR OTHERS

Think positively and be proactive. You never know when you'll be out of work or demoted. If you get laid off, keep looking for a job and never give up. Most places do look for someone who has a degree or a diploma, so if you are lacking education, go back to school and do it now!

29: JOB RELOCATION

Female, Age 61, Senior Occupational Health Nurse

ADVERSITY

The political uncertainty in the area prompted my employer to relocate Head Office to another major city. I literally had no option but to relocate. I informed my employer that I wished to remain, but was refused and literally told that if I did not make the move, I could look for other employment.

This provoked a devastating crisis that affected all areas of my life. There was no option but to stay with the company. I did not want to return to hospital nursing because I found occupational nursing so rewarding. I was older and did not want to jeopardize my retirement income. So I was stuck with this organization.

Personally, I was faced with leaving my friends and relatives. I was so comfortable here. I was settled in my work; I enjoyed my social and community life. Now because of events out of my control, my life was being totally disrupted. I felt upset all the time. My friends got so tired of listening to me, they stopped calling and even refused to support my view that I was being treated unfairly. When I discovered that my new accommodation in the bigger city would be triple the previous rent, I went nuts.

When I arrived in the new city, I was shocked to discover that I was unofficially no longer the senior nurse. I was more or less told that I was not a "valued employee and could easily be replaced." A great way to ease into a relocation!

SELF-DEFEATING THINKING

It's not fair, I have done a good job for the company. Why aren't they doing more to help me?

How could everyone be so insensitive to my needs? How dare they treat me this way!

NEW THINKING

At first I believed that it would simplify matters for everyone if I quit. But I was too stubborn, and I decided that I wasn't going to do that. Then I said to myself that if this is the way the company wants it, then I'll learn to live with it. From now on I'll do only what I have to and no more. My friends told me not to fret, since I was still getting my full salary. Yet I was uncomfortable with this reaction. This was not me. However, these were not normal circumstances either.

EMOTIONAL RESPONSE

My pride was still hurt. I was very cautious with everyone. It's like you don't know who your true allies are in the beginning.

I felt somewhat troubled because I was used to putting out my best—not holding back my performance.

It's interesting how time does heal, because after a while I could live with this situation and was really getting used to it. My blood pressure finally came under control and I even laughed once in a while.

SOLUTION AND OUTCOME

I established a few friendships and was able to unload some of my frustrations. I made a supreme effort to break the ice with the nurse whom I had to work with. I tried to be pleasant to her, and massaged her ego to make her feel more important.

I wanted to get on a level where we could relate more positively. And I totally backed off from the areas that she claimed as hers in the work setting, so she would be less threatened. I accepted a secondary role to make peace.

STICKING WITH IT

I have accepted that this is the way it is going to be, and that it will probably be like this until I retire.

I'm willing to make the best of it. My personal life is in order and I feel more settled now that I have bought a condo. I occasionally go back to visit my friends and relatives and everyone can tell that things are okay with me.

SLIPPING BACK

I remind myself that I'm not willing to put out more for the company. I am willing to do a good job in the areas that I am responsible for and I will keep myself professionally current, but I will not go out of my way to please the company.

I feel that I now understand their policy. It was my own fault for being so naive. I was wrong to assume that they would all appreciate what I've done over the years.

You can't assume that things will be the same. It's better to think a day at a time. Having unrealistic expectations can cause you a lot of grief.

ADVICE FOR OTHERS

I would recommend that anyone in a relocation situation be assertive and demand a face-to-face meeting with all the people involved. Much of the information I got was second or third hand and then when I confronted a particular individual, this person would declare that the information was inaccurate.

Don't expect that other people are always going to come to your aid. You can only ever truly depend on yourself.

Lastly, don't give up. Eventually, things will work out and you learn to look at your problems from a totally different perspective.

30: WORKAHOLISM

Male, Age 59, Teacher

ADVERSITY

Throughout my entire career I have always worked hard and studied hard. As a student growing up with my parents, I remember staying in my room while my friends played outside, and reading and studying my notes so that I could "ace the exam"—and I usually did. Success seemed to come easy. The harder I worked, the more successful I became.

My dream was to become a top-notch teacher. That dream was easily fulfilled. I taught during the daytime at a local high school and in the evening I was an instructor at a college. Teaching wasn't really work to me, it was life itself. Eventually I got married, had two children, and continued to work hard. One day, my wife took the children and walked out on me. For three solid years, I remained depressed.

SELF-DEFEATING THINKING

I thought if I kept working hard everything would be fine. I wasn't having fun like everyone else, but it didn't matter. I got it all done and done well. I reached the top of my profession, was married, and had children. I rarely went out yet I cared for the children, visited family, and worked at two jobs. But when she left, I hit rock bottom. Life didn't matter. For the first time I saw myself as a complete failure. I was boring and a rotten husband and father.

NEW THINKING

First, I got help for my problem and received counselling for about two years. I decided that I was too rigid and too much of a perfectionist. It was important to learn how to live, aside from teaching. The reason for my wife's departure finally became more evident. She simply wanted a more meaningful life, which she found unable to create with me in the picture. Hard reality to come to grips with, but nonetheless true.

EMOTIONAL RESPONSE

I didn't feel so depressed or lonely. In fact I felt more secure in finally knowing who I was and what I needed to do differently.

SOLUTION AND OUTCOME

I began to spend less time with my jobs. I took up tennis, went to church, and visited friends and relatives more often. One day I went to a friend's party and met a lovely lady.

I thought that I better not revert back to my workaholic ways. I needed to learn to be sociable and have fun in my declining years so I could be with this woman.

Now I've learned to decide what work is necessary and what isn't. We spend as much time together as possible, and we make decisions together. I have fun meeting new challenges. I learned to ski so that I could be with her on weekends. Earning a living and getting all of your work done was not the be-all and end-all. Now I lead a more balanced life that includes work and play. Learning to make changes like this doesn't come easily. On occasion I have drifted back into old workaholic habits to avoid stressful new situations.

STICKING WITH IT _____

I review my priorities and make certain that non-work activities are part of them. I always look for creative ways to limit time spent on work and to increase time for socializing and fun.

SLIPPING BACK _____

I tell myself that I cannot always achieve 100 percent perfection, especially if I try to do all of the work on my own. I do the things that are important to me and delegate the rest. Drifting apart from my wife is something I do not wish to repeat now that I am involved with this lovely lady.

ADVICE FOR OTHERS _____

Do your work well but leave time for yourself, family, and friends. Learn other skills besides working. You will have more fun and not end up old and lonely in your retirement years as I could have.

31: LACK OF CONTROL ON THE JOB

Female, Age 31, Industrial Hygienist

ADVERSITY _____

Approximately two years ago, our company was bought out by a major multinational firm. Since that time, various plants have been sold or down-sized and, as a result, certain hygiene staff were let go.

I realized that sooner or later our location would experience some organizational changes, but I hoped that these would not be too dramatic. One day the secretary, operations manager, and I were taken out to lunch by the senior manager to discuss what these structural changes would be.

I was prepared for the message that I would continue to report to the operations manager and that our unit would more or less continue as usual.

My working relationship with this manager was outstanding. Because of his support and my professional programming, we had contributed to the overall health and safety of the employees in our unit.

Out of the blue, the general manager announced that I would be reporting to the human resources manager, an individual who knew nothing about industrial hygiene issues. I was in total disagreement with this decision for ethical, practical, and personal reasons.

This move infuriated me because I simply wasn't included in the decision-making process. I literally had no control over what I'd be doing and who I was to report to. I became so disenchanted and unmotivated that I found it difficult to do almost anything whether it be at work or around the house. I felt alienated from human resources and the management team, as well as betrayed by the head office for not requesting my input before the decision was made. It was difficult to be constructive in planning for a change with which I was in total disagreement.

SELF-DEFEATING THINKING

How could they do this to me? Why didn't they ask my opinion on such a major change? Human resources knew absolutely nothing about industrial hygiene nor were they interested in employee health. The rapport I had tried to build with the employees was going out the window.

My efforts at health and safety promotion would take a back seat to human resource priorities, namely, workers' compensation and disability. Every time human resources said jump, I would have to ask how high. How could the human resources manager even do my performance review? My hopes for a raise in salary were also shattered. It would not be long before I was doing traditional human resources work rather than hygiene work. If I didn't trust the human resources manager, how could I ever respect him enough to report to him? All these thoughts kept going over and over in my mind to the point where I started to develop regular stomach upsets and headaches.

NEW THINKING

I told myself that if I didn't take some control over my destiny, I would really get sick. I raised my concerns with the plant manager who in turn said that he would ask the general manager to reconsider his decision. Then I decided to document my concerns and propose an alternative arrangement with the hope that I might be taken more seriously. If it couldn't be changed, I was determined to have the human resources manager specify certain details in writing, namely my budget, opportunities to attend conferences, date of my performance review, and so forth.

I decided to stay with the company, hope for the best, smile a lot, and concentrate on the needs of the employees. I reminded myself of my accomplishments and the need to keep focused in that direction. I realized that I can't always have a great boss to deal with, and that the job was worth more to me than the quality of this upcoming relationship.

EMOTIONAL RESPONSE

I felt less preoccupied and more goal-oriented. I was stronger and less insecure. Now that I had a plan of action to counteract the decision, or at least deal with it, the sensation of loss of control seemed to disappear.

SOLUTION AND OUTCOME

I got back to doing more things around the house, and was not preoccupied with the job change. I did not stay awake at nights rehashing events in my mind. The physical stress symptoms disappeared and I was able to continue with my responsibilities at work.

STICKING WITH IT

I have received support from key people in my life who have reminded me that I work hard and that I'm strong enough to handle this. I've been around this organization a long time and have developed good rapport with the union, Occupational Health and Safety officials, and the head office. I could go to them for support if I needed to. Additionally, my strong communication skills would come in handy when I disagreed with the human resources manager. The worse that could happen is that he could fire me for disagreeing with him or for challenging his views, and if that happened, I was still employable.

SLIPPING BACK

I start recounting my accomplishments. I remember that the staff at the head office is still there for support and guidance should I require it. I repeatedly tell myself that work isn't everything, and if things don't work out, it isn't the end of the world.

ADVICE FOR OTHERS

Instead of worrying about what might happen once you lose control of your job, take an active part in determining the direction of the changes to take place. Remember that work isn't everything—you can only do the best job you can and that is your only real security. Living day by day makes it easier to ride the tides of change. You may not always be able to work with a great manager, but if you value your work, do your best for the boss you have, you will find that life at work isn't so bad. Finally, seek support from people who are understanding and who will listen—friends, family, close colleagues.

32: JOB INSECURITY DUE TO RESTRUCTURING

Female, Age 57, Social Worker

ADVERSITY

There had been much talk and rumor of change for a number of years but nothing really started to happen until a consultant's report was completed. The recommendation was that a number of small health centers would close but the three largest ones would remain open. There would be some reduction in staff, but it was unclear which permanent staff would be let go. I was the only senior social worker and the fact that I had the third longest service record of all the staff members placed me in a reasonably secure position, as secure as one can be with constant rumors floating around about job terminations and no information about specific plans.

One fateful morning I was called to a meeting with the senior personnel administrator and informed that my position was declared surplus and that if no other position was found by a certain time, I would be released from my responsibilities. Accepting a demotion to join one of the unions was not possible because I was a management employee. I was devastated because I had hoped to retire from this position in six years.

I didn't call my friends; I didn't want to entertain or be entertained. In my tearful and irritable state, I simply wanted to hibernate. It was as though my future had been taken from me. I felt very hurt and depressed because there was a distinct risk that I might lose the work that I had thoroughly enjoyed for over twenty years. Although I was not jealous of others who had greater job security, I was filled with self-pity.

When it came to résumé preparation, I didn't have a clue. Any previous job I had was obtained by word of mouth. Now I was faced with a world that no longer seemed to want me. I labored over the résumé just in case I would need it, but I seemed to be getting nowhere. My good points eluded me, and my bad points and negative thoughts immobilized me.

Work around the house was not getting done. Although my husband and friends were most supportive and reassuring, being told that it was unfair and unfortunate was not enough to influence how I felt.

At work I was tearful on a number of occasions when asked about the uncertainty of my position and my next course of action. Concentrating on tasks was more difficult, although I did manage to do my job, but not with the same enthusiasm and intensity.

Those colleagues with whom I worked most closely were very sympathetic and upset and believed that this was unfair. One of my colleagues offered me the names of a labor lawyer and financial advisor just in case they were needed, which was appreciated.

SELF-DEFEATING THINKING

Why was I so unlucky? Why now when I was nearly sixty years old . . . ? Nobody would want to hire someone my age. I wanted to do another job, but I was not being allowed to. Why after so many years of service was I being so unfairly treated, not being permitted the opportunity of taking a union job just because I was in a management category. I couldn't retire now! If I had to retire or was released at my present age, I would receive considerably less money per month than if I was sixty years of age. To place me in such an insecure and unstable position was so unjust and unfair.

NEW THINKING

If I continued with these destructive thoughts I would make myself sick— maybe even get cancer. My father and two of his sisters died of cancer around my age and that terrified me. I told myself to pull together my spiritual strength and face this adversity. I started to conjure up some new scenarios. Maybe if I lost my job, it would be nice to have more leisure time to do more things around the house. Maybe we could manage on a lesser pension when the time came. If I could continue to believe in myself and counteract the negative, cynical thinking, I knew I would feel better. The support and encouragement from my husband throughout this mess were comforting and reassuring.

EMOTIONAL RESPONSE

I felt more in control, less tense, and less stressed. My predicament seemed more manageable. Also, my headaches occurred less frequently. Self-defeat was replaced with optimism and renewed self-esteem. Maybe I could get another job if I needed to!

SOLUTION AND OUTCOME

I actually started to pursue job opportunities with some other agencies just in case things didn't work out well and I was asked to leave. The heavy weight on my shoulders had been lifted and my concentration returned. It seemed that I finally had prepared myself for the worst and was dealing with everything in a realistic manner, free from self-pity, negativity, and inactivity.

STICKING WITH IT

I am more open about my problem. I talk to others about it without becoming upset and tearful. I repeat over and over again that "it's not the end of the world." Also, I am committed to the beliefs that I could retire if I had to and that I could do work that I didn't like. What is most fascinating is that I accept things that I thought unthinkable before.

SLIPPING BACK

When I think of negative scenarios and I get panicky or I start feeling sorry for myself, I say, "Stop it, it doesn't have to be that way." I then continue to pursue my job search by expanding my network of contacts. Also, I continue to jump into my work and do the best I can, knowing that it may or may not continue.

ADVICE FOR OTHERS

Limit the time you allow yourself to wallow in self-pity. Think about your possible scenarios and try to consider as many alternatives as you can. Realize your negative thoughts are destructive to your self-esteem. Don't wait for jobs to come to you, actively seek contacts and new prospects, just in case you need them. If you have any spiritual supports, use them. And finally, realize that how you think determines whether you win or you lose.

33: BEING CRITICIZED IN FRONT OF COLLEAGUES

Female, Age 36, Human Resources Supervisor

ADVERSITY

As a human resources supervisor, I was accustomed to reporting to the vice-president of human resources, who was a reasonable, thoughtful professional who listened well and was committed to establishing a strong and respectable department. However, because of a major reorganization my reporting relationship changed. I now was expected to report to a divisional human resources manager with whom I always had difficulty. He was very chauvinistic, accusatory, and easily threatened by women, especially those who outperformed him. Rumors had already started that he had it in for me, and that sooner or later we would come to blows. Sure enough at a staff meeting, halfway through the agenda, he started to attack. In front of my colleagues, he accused me of being very insecure as a woman, of being inadequate in "a man's world" as evidenced by my short hair, and of being a marginal performer in my role as human resources supervisor.

This really shook me up, especially the statement that my performance was inadequate. I can't remember the last time I was rattled. My family quickly came to my rescue and were very encouraging in an attempt to boost my confidence. Fascinatingly, my children were most surprised that their mother had these hassles and obstacles to overcome at work, because these were similar to what they had to deal with at school.

At work, I found myself avoiding my manager because I had lost all respect for him due to his inappropriate and unprofessional actions. Fortunately, my peers rallied around me and expressed their deep concern about the manager's rude behavior.

SELF-DEFEATING THINKING

I screamed inside that he had no right to treat me this way. I would never display any loyalty again. How could someone in his position behave in such a rude, callous, disparaging manner? A pig, that's what he was, a pig!

NEW THINKING

As a result of lengthy discussions with family, friends, and peers, I came to the conclusion that if he wanted to remain unprofessional, obnoxious, and a poor example of a human resources manager, so be it. He was responsible for his conduct and his destructive behavior. In addition, I took stock of what I had accomplished since I joined human resources and it was quite impressive. Many of my colleagues reminded me of the contributions I had made and the good will that I had created. Also, I made up my mind not to resort to similar tactics in dealing with this manager. Under no circumstances would I lower myself to that level.

EMOTIONAL RESPONSE

I felt sorry for the manager whom I now viewed as a pathetic representation of human resources. There was a strong sense of determination to eventually sit down with him and constructively voice my concern.

SOLUTION AND OUTCOME _____

I sat down with my manager and gently yet firmly discussed the confrontation episode at the staff meeting. We discussed how to prevent similar episodes from occurring, and eventually came away understanding one another more. It was apparent to me that our working relationship would probably remain somewhat strained. My present position in human resources would not be the only and remaining one, so I knew that I could tolerate him.

STICKING WITH IT _____

I remind myself that this is not the last manager in my career. If I managed this jerk and his silly actions, then I could handle most situations. There would be other interesting career opportunities in the future!

SLIPPING BACK _____

Who gives a shit?

ADVICE FOR OTHERS _____

Don't put the blame on the person who has confronted you, but put it down to their lack of control or poor professional ethics. Don't be hasty in making decisions, especially those that involve quitting. Discuss the situation with trusted colleagues who might lend good advice to help you work through the problem.

34: BOREDOM/LACK OF CHALLENGE

Male, Age 48, President, Car Dealership

ADVERSITY _____

While working as a vocational teacher, I experienced the following problems:
(a) lack of financial resources to do the job, (b) lack of continuing education

to keep up to date to do the job, (c) lack of support from the administration, which was academically oriented whereas I was technically oriented. The administration had no real interest in continuing our program—they preferred putting money into their own pet projects. The class size was too big, which translated into many discipline problems, and wouldn't you know it, there was no support from administration and parents to improve matters. All of these factors led to my frustration with "the system." The challenge of the job had disappeared; the repetitiveness of fighting the system was simply overwhelming. The outlook for the future—more of the same.

I coped by doing the best I could, yet I found it a chore to get up in the morning. Thoughts of going to work were depressing and I simply could not wait for the day to end. When I'd see the kids come through the door each morning, they represented the enmity of my occupation. I wouldn't welcome them, I nearly despised them. The last straw, which broke the camel's back, was the combination of a "stress attack" and a severe migraine headache that required medical attention.

There was no *joie de vivre* in my personal life. I was spiritless, my job was boring and meaningless, and each day was a repeat of the previous day.

SELF-DEFEATING THINKING

For me, it was a matter of not having enough push to leave. I thought things might get better. One day, I'd say that I have to get out of here; the next day, I'd believe that the predicament might somehow turn around. I was waiting for the right opportunity to come walking through the door and present itself to me, instead of actively seeking work on my own. I kept waffling back and forth and was afraid to make up my mind. In essence, I was procrastinating.

NEW THINKING

When I had the stress attack, I decided that life was too short, that when things start affecting your health, it's time to start looking elsewhere. It's funny how all of a sudden, your priorities become clearer.

I decided I wasn't going to wait for something better to present itself, but rather, I was going to simply start looking. It wasn't going to be easy and there were risks that I might be unemployed for a time, but that wasn't as important as making the move to leave. The one-year severance package that I received helped to ease my financial worries considerably.

EMOTIONAL RESPONSE

For the first time in a long time I felt challenged, free, adventuresome, younger, energized, and in control.

SOLUTION AND OUTCOME

Based on my automotive experience, I decided to check out car dealerships. Interviews were carried out with many people until I bought a business. I wasn't any wealthier, but I had greater respect for myself. Over time, I was exposed to hundreds of people whom I would never have met had I remained stuck in the classroom. Now I feel like I'm making a contribution. People seek me out and value my advice, where previously I was avoided. The set of problems I have because of the business I'm in have a chance of being solved, whereas previously problems would persist because of the bureaucracy.

STICKING WITH IT

Hard work. Now I attack problems on a day-to-day basis, face up to challenges, and move ahead.

SLIPPING BACK

I go out looking for more problems, more challenges, more opportunities. If I'm not selling cars, I determine ways to rent them. I find myself constantly looking for something new, trying to uncover a new approach. Boredom, frustration, and lack of challenges are no longer part of my life.

ADVICE FOR OTHERS

Look for another job or career. Examine newspapers, send out applications, go for interviews. Identify your personal strengths and skills and seek out people to whom you can talk about your capabilities and possible career opportunities. Keep repeating these steps until you find something you like. You'll always be successful if you like what you're doing and are allowed to do it.

THE WORKPLACE SOLUTION

The work world is caught up in a flurry of change, the likes of which we have not seen before. Industries are repositioning in an effort to become more competitive. Technological advancement is progressing at such a fast pace that what was prominent yesterday is outdated today. Because of the increased use of computers, greater and heavier demands are being placed upon people with unwavering regularity. Organizational realignments, restructuring, down-sizing, right-sizing are becoming everyday occurrences. Mergers, acquisitions, and joint ventures are also directions in which companies are going in an effort to tackle the global marketplace.

Corporate cultures are shifting. No longer is the "top-down" approach to management so appropriate; instead, managers are becoming leaders and coaches and employees are gaining more say in their day-to-day operations. As work becomes more demanding, employees become more demanding. People want more say in what they do, they want more meaningful work, they want a more reasonable balance between home and work, and they want to make a greater contribution. Women are competing more effectively in the marketplace and they are demanding more from their companies. Single-parent families are no longer a rarity. Minority groups are making their presence felt in companies. Senior management is now realizing that older people's skills and experience are critical in deciding which direction a company should take, and consequently, these workers are needed more than ever. Many people are dedicated to their work, but at the same time, they are constrained by child care issues, parental care issues, concern about maintaining a reasonable marital relationship.

Amidst these transformations are more compelling changes at the level of the individual employee. There exists a quiet but determined effort on the part of certain employees to maintain a balance between their work and their health, happiness, and productivity. This movement is represented here by the "miracle makers" who just described their struggles with and ultimate triumphs over adversity. They used strategies that transformed problems into more positive experiences.

The business community would be wise to fully appreciate the process of overcoming adversity as illustrated by the preceding interviews, because as the tides of change continue, many employees will be negatively affected and may not be well equipped to deal with the workplace problems that arise. Furthermore, business leaders would be prudent to institute specific training programs founded on the experiences of the miracle makers, to inoculate all employees, both management and staff, against the possible ravages of an ever-changing workplace. Our miracle makers used a variety of thinking strategies to confront a range of work-related problems—and they were all able to turn their lives around.

These people challenged what went on in their heads. They shifted their mindsets; they altered their perspectives. They were not prepared to settle for a philosophy of life that was not in the best interests of their health, happiness and productivity. Once they made the necessary cognitive shifts, they were then primed for the next phase—problem resolution. They were propelled into action to make their working lives dramatically better.

According to our miracle makers, they were originally focused on thinking that got them into a mess at work—and then kept them in a mess at work, which eventually spilled over into other parts of their lives. This kind of thinking—that person does not appreciate me, I'm a failure, I must be stupid, I'm afraid to take risks, I'll never make it—completely immobilized these people at first. Then something happened, not *to* them but *inside* them, that turned their thinking around. They were able to gather their inner resources to stake a claim on happiness and well-being no matter what direction external forces took. Their thinking became more flexible, less self-defeating—not everyone in this world has to like me, I refuse to spend too much time worrying, I will focus on what I need to do rather than how others should be treating me, I don't have to be everything to everyone, I acknowledge my limitations.

Ask yourself this? If you had a chance to commit yourself to a particular line of reasoning, which one would it be? The former or the latter? Well, the answer is obvious. The answer is obvious, not only because it feels better to have the latter perspective, but more important, this line of reasoning prepares you for problem-solving.

I am not suggesting a simple solution here. However, I am positing a particular approach that will help with various workplace challenges. And our miracle makers certainly attest to the effectiveness of this approach.

If you are committed to a more logical, rational, flexible, tolerant, patient, and optimistic way of thinking, more than likely your problem will be managed and managed well, your productivity will be enhanced and your health and happiness will improve. In fact, you may become your own miracle maker in the workplace.

PART 2

On the Home Front

35: CARE OF A PARENT

Female, Age 39, Financial Analyst

ADVERSITY

My mother had a stroke while I was working up north. I had to return to the city to help my dad look after her.

I had to sell my house and quit my job and it was very hard to give these up. While I was attending to my mother, I took the opportunity to further my education and acquired a masters degree in business administration. Shortly after my graduation, my mother passed away. My father was devastated and I had to stay on to give him comfort and support. In the meantime, I was offered a position in another city and I accepted. Each day I had to commute between the two cities to meet domestic and occupational demands.

During this period, I had to spend a total of four hours per day traveling. I certainly did not have much of a personal life.

Every day after work I would rush to catch the bus and then the train, in order to be home to prepare dinner for my dad. Then we would spend a little time watching television or just chatting before retiring for the night.

With so little spare time left, I did not visit relatives or friends as often as I would have liked. It came to a point where I was discouraging them from visiting or calling me. Some of them understood, but others did not and I felt guilty about it.

Sometimes when there was a lot of work to do, I could not stay after work to get more done just because I had to get home.

Being an important member of the team at work, I would have liked to socialize with my co-workers more. Again, I could not do so because my father was waiting for me. Most of my colleagues were rather understanding.

SELF-DEFEATING THINKING

My thoughts were rather cynical and negative. The commuting was ruining me. I objected to what was happening. Why did my mother have to die? Why was my father so dependent? Why was I the only one he could rely upon? Why were my two brothers away in different parts of the country? Why did I not have another sister to share this load with me? If it was not for this family burden, I could live closer to my workplace. Then I would not be wasting so much time on traveling and I would not be so tired. I would have more time to myself and enjoy the company of my friends. When would all of this end? If I didn't stop traveling back and forth, my career would be ruined.

NEW THINKING

My breakthrough was realizing that father could survive, even without the same attention he had received from me. Second, and more important, I realized that my commuting was so problematic because I resented being the sole caregiver in my father's life, not necessarily because I was driving four hours a day. If I helped him find new interests, maybe he would not be as dependent on me. When he begins to establish other companionships, he may not need me by his side all the time. Then I could have my own home and have my own life once more. I may not have to commute daily ever again! It finally hit home that I didn't have to fulfil all of his needs while watching my own needs dry up.

EMOTIONAL RESPONSE

I felt the burden lifted somewhat and I was hopeful about having a life of my own again.

SOLUTION AND OUTCOME

I communicated to my father for the first time that commuting four hours each day was putting a tremendous strain on my life and my career. Also, I stated that I had faith that my father didn't really need all of the attention that I was showering on him.

I encouraged father to join some clubs and to have other companions. Eventually he met a fine lady and became engaged to her. Knowing that soon he would be married again, I started to look for accommodation elsewhere and was lucky to find an apartment close to work.

STICKING WITH IT

I realized that I alone was carrying a burden unnecessarily. I truly was convinced that father could not survive without me and therefore pressured myself to commute four hours each day. When father announced that he was to be married again, I discussed with him my plan to leave and that he would be well looked after by his future wife. He was sad but grateful that I sacrificed my time for him. Now I am living in my own home, cooking my own meals, enjoying my own friends, socializing and loving it!

SLIPPING BACK

There were times when I felt obliged to be with father more often and would postpone the work and the outings that I had planned. I would remind myself that he had someone to look after him now, that he would be fine, and that I didn't have to place extraordinary demands on myself just to prove what I could do for him.

ADVICE FOR OTHERS

Examine what you are doing and why you are doing it. Sometimes what appears to be an obvious problem, like commuting long distances, is not so simple, but is complicated by other dynamics, like trying to prove you are a "wonderful daughter"!

36: DEATH OF A SPOUSE

Female, Age 28, Real Estate Agent

ADVERSITY

My husband, a police officer, was killed in the line of duty. I was 9 months pregnant and our daughter was twenty months old.

My husband was working on the night shift because of unrest and recent police shootings. Therefore, I had more anxiety about him being at work and was afraid that something would happen. I feared his friends coming to my door with terrible news.

Earlier that night I had expressed my fears that he could be killed, that it could actually happen to him.

When the police came to the door, it was like a nightmare, because I knew their method of notifying relatives. The actual event seemed like a hazy dream.

It changed everything in my life; plans for myself and my children were turned upside down. Any expectation for an exciting future vanished. The loneliness, although I had my children, was overpowering. When you love someone and he or she is suddenly snatched, well it's not comparable to anything I know.

It dramatically affected my family life with the children. I had to become more independent, more handy around the house, more in charge of all our affairs. Having a big extended family made the transition somewhat easier, because of their willingness to help.

The media was very hard to deal with. The police association, well they kept saying different things about my entitlement to the benefits. These were very awkward times. Because my husband was a police officer, there was a constant stream of his friends coming through the house. However, it inevitably stopped, and the house was filled with a strong sense of abandonment.

SELF-DEFEATING THINKING

I thought I was totally in control. Then I realized I wasn't. Or it appeared that I was—people thought I was so strong.

There were moments when I was so lonely and depressed that I wanted to run away.

When I was told about the death, I totally denied it. It took me the longest time to understand how someone could be dead in an instant. I couldn't accept that. Death couldn't be that fast.

Then, it became difficult to go out in public places like a mall or a restaurant. I'd see families together and thought that's the way my life should be.

I couldn't watch T.V. shows or commercials—anything that showed Mom, Dad, and the kids. I was denied that, it was taken away from me.

NEW THINKING

I came to an acceptance of the circumstances, no one else would do it for me if I didn't. I made the choice to carry on, to get up every day, to raise the kids, to go forward.

I had to progress from the day it happened, my new baby and my daughter were counting on me. There had to be strength there for them, otherwise I could have wallowed in self-pity for a long time.

Time helped me to change. The first thing I was able to concentrate on was country music, because it was so different from what "we" had listened to, together.

Having my son was a turning point, because my priorities became crystal clear. I needed to be there for my kids and therefore I couldn't fall apart.

EMOTIONAL RESPONSE

I think time heals the pain of loss. The more time goes by, the better it seems to be.

I felt better. Once you start to cope and things run smoothly, you feel proud that you survived. I felt that if I could live through this, I could live through anything.

SOLUTION AND OUTCOME

Now I was a single mother. I accepted that I might always be a single mother, although this was not my first choice. Also, I was thankful for my son and daughter and for the security we now had as a unit.

STICKING WITH IT

Well another man entered my life and I remarried.

It's nice now because I have someone else, I'm able to rely on someone, I'm also needed. This loss taught me to appreciate more, and to fully realize that things can be taken away. I don't take it for granted that my new husband will always be there. My biggest fear is that I'll lose him and have to go through it again. What has now become clear is to avoid squabbling about trivial matters and focus on the important things we have together.

SLIPPING BACK

I slip back to the fear of being married and losing my husband again. When I tell this to my husband, he says "Don't be silly!"

Sometimes I really have to control this obsession and say "what will be, will be," I can't keep worrying or it takes over and I become somber and melancholy.

Psychologically I have to talk to myself and coax myself to snap out of it. I try to be thankful for every day, and I'd rather have the time with my husband, however long, than not at all.

As the saying goes, "Better to have loved and lost, then never to have loved at all."

ADVICE FOR OTHERS

It'll get better, it takes time. Wounds do heal. You can have a life again. Don't lose faith. Take one day at a time.

37: SEPARATION AND DIVORCE

Female, Age 50, Vice President of a Financial Company

ADVERSITY

It started off with financial difficulties, then our respective interests began to shift. Philosophically and politically we began to develop completely different outlooks on what we wanted in life and for the future.

Over the space of 3–4 months, he quite often went out late at night, supposedly visiting a friend. Together we didn't do that much anymore. At the time he was also going to school to finish another degree. I entirely trusted him and never doubted what he said. One day he declared that he was having an affair with a woman whom we knew. I asked him what he was going to do and whether he was leaving. He didn't know what to do and was virtually undecided.

He stayed in our home for the next 3–4 days, but was at her home every evening. Finally I called her house and told him to come right home and make a decision one way or the other. I couldn't exist with him and this affair. He did eventually leave.

Personally, I think I was in a vacuum for a while. I wasn't his wife anymore, but I wasn't myself either.

My seven-year-old child, who worshipped her father, was devastated. Interestingly enough she became very sympathetic towards me, was very concerned, and always tried to help me. I was worried that she was becoming the mother and I was the child. Financially, I was still working and making the same money, but I didn't have the drain of his university bills to pay. So I was able to maintain our reasonable standard of living.

My very good friends were supportive, but they had always been. A lot of them came forward and I guess I realized how close they were to me. I had always been close to my family so nothing there really changed.

My work was affected. On the job, I felt that I could break down into tears at any given moment, and because of my responsible position, matters were that much more awkward and embarrassing. Fortunately, my supervisors were understanding, terrific, and really went above and beyond anything employers should ever have to do. However, I knew I needed the job. I wasn't getting any child support, alimony, or anything like that, so I was determined to hang in there.

Socially, I found myself becoming closer to some single people in our organization, and I began to spend time with them outside of work.

SELF-DEFEATING THINKING

I guess I went the full gambit. I remember thinking I should kill myself because my life wasn't worth living anymore. I thought that when I made my marriage vows it was forever. Then I realized that's stupid. I have this child and I can't abandon her. Then I became consumed with the way in which I was going to get along, having to pay bills, taking care of the house, and everything else. But I realized that I had been doing this for eight years of our marriage. Next I wondered about my failings as a woman being the prime reason for the marriage breakdown. Was it me? Did I lack something? Was I a sexual misfit? Boy can your mind ever turn your spirits inside out!

NEW THINKING

I wasn't going to allow anyone to make me unhappy or destroy me, I was going to make the very best of my life.

EMOTIONAL RESPONSE

A lot better. Also, a lot better about him. I didn't resent him as much. I could look at him differently, actually see his good points, and appreciate the time we had in our marriage.

SOLUTION AND OUTCOME

Basically, I became much more of an individual. I started dating, making decisions, and feeling free.

STICKING WITH IT

I remarried. I met someone who was the perfect type of man for me. He let me be the individual I'd become; he didn't try to hold me back. He didn't force his will on me in any way. Yet if I wanted his strength or shoulder, it was always there for me.

SLIPPING BACK

With my first marriage, I should have said something when I saw things not working properly, but I didn't. Now I yell on occasion, I don't put up with the bullshit, I don't let myself get pushed around. I have my own feelings and ideas, and I try to verbalize them.

ADVICE FOR OTHERS

I see a lot of people going through divorce who literally poison themselves with hate, with regrets, and with recriminations against the other person. They only destroy themselves and their children. Don't say horrible things about the other person to the children. They are going to love the other parent even with faults, regardless of what happened in the marriage. All you're going to do is create bad feelings with your children, which also may reflect very negatively on you and your ambitions as the primary caregiver.

38: DIFFICULT PREGNANCY/ CHILDBIRTH

Female, Age 27, Interior Designer

ADVERSITY

Being married a year, we had just bought our first home, and I was pregnant with our first child. Everything had gone well throughout the pregnancy. I was one week overdue and my specialist was sending me for a non-stress test to determine if everything was alright. My appointment was the next morning. During the test the nurse told me that the baby's heartbeat was irregular, very fast, skipping a few beats only to go very low. My specialist was called in. He didn't come right out and say anything definite, but I could tell that he was concerned. I was to remain in hospital to be monitored. If I didn't go into labor on my own, or the baby became more distressed, induction or possibly a C-section would be necessary.

I went into labor that evening at about 7:30 P.M. They gave me my epidural the next morning and labor seemed to stop. Then they induced me. Doctors came and went, never staying quite long enough for any questions to be asked. At 10:00 P.M. the next evening I was examined again and was finally dilated fully. The doctor then informed me that the baby was coming face up instead of face down. He would have to give me a heavy dose of epidural; try to spread my pelvis a little more, as it seemed the baby had become wedged; use forceps to turn the baby; and attempt delivery. At this point I told him I didn't care I just wanted this ordeal over with. At 10:30 P.M. we proceeded to the delivery room with a number of people, including my husband, mother, my specialist, three nurses, three residents, and two anesthesiologists. After a great deal of work on almost everyone's part, our son was born, 28 hours after labor started. They left the baby with my husband and me for an hour and then took him off to the neonatal ICU to be monitored. I was then taken to my room two floors away.

The next morning I went to inquire as to his condition. The staff on my floor couldn't give me any information and told me if I wanted to know I would have to go up to the unit. This seemed almost impossible. It took me ten minutes just to get to the desk, now they wanted me to walk to the far end of the hall and go up two floors. I thought I did well walking as far as I did! When I did get up to the unit the neonatal specialist was there and informed me that the baby had been examined by three specialists and did not have any cardiac problems. The baby was to remain in the unit because he was refusing to take a bottle and they would have to use alternate methods. I had wanted to breast feed but I didn't know what the baby's status was. I went back to the other floor when he was due to be fed and tried breast feeding. It was successful and when they decided that he was receiving adequate nutrition, they released him from ICU to the floor nursery. The rest of our hospital stay was uneventful.

SELF-DEFEATING THINKING

From the time I realized that something could be wrong during the non-stress test until that baby was in the regular nursery, I was terrified. I mistrusted the staff, thinking they weren't telling me everything. I thought I was a failure as a parent even before I became one. All my joyous expectations flew out the window. I had an empty feeling and thoughts of doom. I remember pleading with God to let the baby live, that no matter what was wrong with it, I would look after it and be a good parent. I wanted to shut everyone out. I tried to stay calm, but I would no sooner get relaxed and those butterflies in my stomach would get loose. What was I going to do and how was I going to react if this baby was not okay? After he was born I wanted to feel happy, but I was hesitant because something could still be wrong with him.

The next morning when I was on my way up to the unit, the walk seemed long in more ways than one. I wanted to go, but I didn't want to go. There was something wrong and they weren't going to tell me until I got up there. I was almost sick to my stomach before I got up to the unit. When the baby was refusing to be bottle fed, I told myself that he was probably just as exhausted as I was. Throughout this entire episode, there was an overriding sense of fear and doom that troubled me considerably.

NEW THINKING

In labor and delivery I remember feeling detached, almost like a spectator, watching and observing the people around me, trying to read their faces, looking for signs in their eyes. I kept thinking if there was something really wrong with the baby they would not leave him with me this long. They would take the baby. Don't lose control. No matter what the problem is, I can handle it. When the baby was finally born, they checked him over and there was no initial look of concern on their faces. The doctor then assured me that they were only taking the baby to the unit for observation.

EMOTIONAL RESPONSE

Each time we progressed a little further in this process, I felt more and more relief. I seemed to be getting stronger, more determined, more in control. After this was all over I felt I could handle just about anything.

SOLUTION AND OUTCOME

I had more serious complications with my third pregnancy and delivery. This time I had more people depending on me. I had a two-year-old and a four-year-old at home. I still felt scared, but calm at the same time. I kept my emotions in check because I had questions that I needed answers to. If I didn't stay in control, I wouldn't be able to process information. We made it through that pregnancy, labor, and delivery.

STICKING WITH IT

The difficult pregnancy was an unfamiliar situation for me, but once dealt with, I had a knowledge base from which to draw on. When it occurred, I found that initially there was fear and panic. I don't think that was unreasonable, but I didn't give in to it so the problem never took over. This approach has helped me immensely with other difficulties in my life. Now when an issue arises, I give it some thought, pull it apart, piece it together, and consider alternatives. I then discuss the issue with my husband and we bounce it around. If there is no solution, I don't worry about it; if there is a solution, I go after it. Also, I usually ask myself if this same problem will bother me as much tomorrow, then I shelve it till the next day and see if it bothers me as much. On the other hand, if the issue pertains directly to me, my family, or our happiness then I deal with it immediately.

SLIPPING BACK

When I begin to feel overwhelmed, I ask myself, "Is this significant? Is it worth the panic and fear you are creating?" I sometimes talk out loud when dealing with a problem, or I talk it over with my husband. He really is a very good listener.

ADVICE FOR OTHERS

To begin with, I believe there was only ever one woman who had a textbook pregnancy and delivery, and the only place you can find her is in a textbook. You can't do anything until you know what the problem is. Then if you can change it, change it, if not, let it ride. In the light of adversity, maintain your cool, and *always* hold on to hope.

39: PLACING A PARENT IN A RETIREMENT HOME

Female, Age 61, Politician

ADVERSITY

My mother, who had previously been very active, was losing her eyesight. She couldn't see to shop, and she could become easily separated from me when I took her anywhere. Her personal hygiene was deteriorating because she couldn't notice the stains and the dirt on her clothing. Unable to go out on her own, the quality of her life was rapidly deteriorating. What kept her occupied were her talking books, her cribbage club, and her soap operas. She was becoming more isolated and self-centered, particularly about her health and bodily functions. Although there was no tension at home because of an understanding husband, my relationships with my brothers and sisters were very strained because mother was playing both ends against the middle. She became demanding of us and would even call me at work to bitterly complain about her other children who were "mistreating her."

SELF-DEFEATING THINKING

Because of my mother playing one sibling against the other in terms of who said what, I developed a tremendous amount of guilt and animosity towards my sisters and brothers. A lot of time and energy was spent in checking out stories and getting things straight. I repeated over and over again that they had no right to treat her this way. Yet when I got the true picture, my mother was often the instigator. Then guilt would overwhelm me for thinking that my siblings were the culprits. The sleepless nights were becoming more frequent. Because I was the oldest, I firmly believed that it was my responsibility to maintain family harmony, and since that wasn't happening, I was at fault.

NEW THINKING

I began to realize that my mother was fighting to maintain some control, and that the old folks whom I had ever admired were really the feisty ones, as opposed to those who sat and did nothing. I also put some of her behavior down to organic brain disease, which was later confirmed by our family doctor. So I stopped the self-blame and refused to get angry with my brothers and sisters. I accepted that mother really wouldn't want to create bad family relations. So I brought the siblings together to agree that we wouldn't accept mother's version of a story until we had checked it out with each other first. Those of us who were able took mother to Florida in the winter so that we could observe and assess her. Later we decided that a retirement home was indicated, but until we could place her, we would arrange for "Meals on Wheels" and a homecare worker.

EMOTIONAL RESPONSE

I felt better and more optimistic that the siblings could agree and work together to ensure that mother was properly cared for. However, the job of telling her about a retirement home was left in my hands. I had to plan the best way of approaching the issue.

SOLUTION AND OUTCOME

I planned the steps carefully. I explained to mother that we would keep her in her home as long as possible with the help we were arranging, but that she must prepare for the day when this would no longer be enough. I took her to inspect the retirement home and then placed her name on the waiting list. Mother seemed to take everything in stride, mainly because so much attention was being paid to her. However, after a few days, she rebelled at the idea. But I remained patient yet firm. I told her repeatedly that her health and well-being were our prime concern. A couple of months later, she was admitted to the retirement home, although she did resist somewhat.

STICKING WITH IT

I try to keep a sense of humor about things and try to keep things in perspective. I have gotten on with other serious problems in life and I was certain that I would manage this one.

SLIPPING BACK

I accept the fact that you always second-guess yourself. I have some regrets about what I have done with my mother, but she is in great hands. I tell myself that the problem won't go away, but it is under control.

ADVICE FOR OTHERS

Communicate. Communicate. Communicate. Try to have patience. Realize that there are frustrations in life, but that things can always be worse. Cry a lot. Don't be afraid of your emotions.

40: SUICIDE IN THE FAMILY

Female, Age 51, Auditor

ADVERSITY

It was the middle of the night when I received a call that my sister-in-law had committed suicide. She had shot herself. We had been childhood friends and had remained close friends up until she and my brother had separated two years ago. I had not had contact with her since then. We were 1200 miles apart and seemed to go our separate ways. She had been a prominent psychologist who was very involved in child abuse cases and women's organizations, especially those that dealt with assault on women. She had numerous papers published and had done some work on documentaries. I was in a state of disbelief. This woman seemed to have so much going for her. I flew to the east coast a few days later for the funeral. After the funeral I learned that this suicide had been planned for a number of months. She had left all the documentation for her funeral arrangements, a letter for each one of her children, a journal, and even a quarter that she had borrowed. Also, I learned that when the oldest daughter was home in the summer from university, the two of them had sat down and watched a film on suicide and carried on a discussion afterwards. Her daughter had told her mother that she felt suicide to be the highest form of self-hatred. Since this type of discussion was not uncommon, the daughter did not think this exchange to be strange or reason for concern. Several days later when the daughter was leaving to return to school, her mother gave her some jewelery to take with her. This too was not uncommon.

A few days after the funeral, I returned home and tried to carry on with my life. When the will was read I was informed by my brother that the jewelery, originally given to his daughter, was left to me. Initially, I refused the jewelery, but the daughter no longer wanted it, so it was sent to me. It

95

now sits in a safety deposit box. The rest of my sister-in-law's estate was left to the women's organizations. The oldest daughter is now contesting the will, not because she believes that she is entitled to the estate, but as a matter of principle. For some reason she holds these groups responsible for her mother's death.

SELF-DEFEATING THINKING

I was very upset and disturbed that this person whom I thought I knew, would take her life. I was guilt-ridden about not staying in touch with her, that maybe if I had remained close I could have been there for her. Her children would probably go through hell and I was angry that she thought her action would do this to them. For a period of time around the funeral, I was literally numb.

NEW THINKING

It helped that I had attended the funeral as I had the opportunity to talk to the other members of my family and try to understand what had been going on in her life. It was from conversations with people who were close to her that I realized how much torment she indeed was experiencing. I then acknowledged that neither I nor anyone else could have made a real difference. She was committed to ending it all and she was successful.

EMOTIONAL RESPONSE

I felt like a weight had been lifted although I have my down days when I feel angry with her. My emotions still ride the roller coaster.

SOLUTION AND OUTCOME

I take time to enjoy life. We get so busy and so caught up, we don't take time for the things that are really important.

STICKING WITH IT

At times I have difficulty understanding why she took her life, and I don't think enough time has passed for all my emotions to settle down. There are still so many unanswered questions. Maybe when her journal is published (a publisher has decided to print it), some of these questions will be answered.

SLIPPING BACK

I tell myself that I am not accountable or responsible for the decisions of others and that includes my sister-in-law.

I feel those who attempt suicide and are successful have formulated the willful intent to die. No one else should assume the blame for their actions.

41: CRIME AGAINST FAMILY HOME

Female, Age 40, Professor

ADVERSITY

One evening I entered the hallway of my apartment building and encountered my neighbor and a policeman investigating several apartment break-ins. My own apartment was then examined after it was discovered that the lock had been destroyed. The rooms were ransacked, and many personal belongings were taken, including family keepsakes, watches, wedding and engagement rings. I felt invaded and violated because an outsider had pried into my private life. Every evening a feeling of terror overcame me as I walked into my empty apartment. For a long time, before going to bed I would thoroughly search the place, including the cupboards, behind the curtains, under the bed. I could only sleep on my back, so there was a clear view of the front door.

SELF-DEFEATING THINKING

Thinking about the burglary did not surface during busy working hours, but the moment I was alone in my quiet apartment the worrisome thoughts would recur. "It's going to happen again." "He is lurking around." These and other thoughts wouldn't leave me. When I saw strangers pass by my building, I would wonder if any of them was the robber. Also, I would try to imagine what the intruder looked like. I actually gave "him a face." This made matters 100 percent worse.

NEW THINKING

I didn't know what to think anymore. Then one night, while sitting by myself, I said that this incident is like lightning, it would probably only strike once in the same place. There was no reason for this person to return. I couldn't understand why I hadn't reasoned this way earlier.

EMOTIONAL RESPONSE

The imaginary faces began to fade and my sense of control seemed to return.

SOLUTION AND OUTCOME

I generally became more comfortable, especially in the evenings, and I could even enjoy being in the apartment alone.

STICKING WITH IT

By comparing my problem to other people's difficulties, I began to realize how insignificant this was. Although I don't buy much jewelry for myself anymore, I have started to decorate my apartment again.

SLIPPING BACK

When I find myself being compulsive, by checking my apartment at night, I tell myself to keep things in perspective. Also, sometimes when I am afraid to go down to the basement, I simply force myself to do it and tolerate the nervousness although I do turn on a light in the corner. This reoccurrence happens every few months, but it's slowly disappearing.

ADVICE FOR OTHERS

My advice is to keep things in perspective. Be grateful that family members weren't threatened and that only material objects that can be replaced were taken.

Another robbery happened to me about 1½ years later, but this time around, I did not have the same emotional reaction although I was angry. I ended up leaving the apartment not because I was distraught, but rather, I hated my things being destroyed.

42: DAUGHTER LEAVING HOME

Female, Age 49, Veterinarian

ADVERSITY

My daughter and I had a very close and wonderful relationship. I had brought up my two children without a father because my husband and I had been separated soon after my second child was born. I worked very hard to support myself and my two kids, making sure that they had the best that I could afford. My daughter was sent to dancing school and for piano lessons and other activities she enjoyed. She always had good health and enjoyed life. As she grew up we grew closer. I encouraged her to be open and honest in all things.

She was now 19 years old and had a boyfriend who lived out of town. It was brought to my attention that her boyfriend was in for the weekend. This particular weekend my daughter requested to stay with her girlfriend. Knowing that the boyfriend was in town, I became suspicious and phoned the girlfriend requesting to speak to my daughter, only to be told that she had not been there at all. I immediately panicked because I now believed my suspicions about her spending the weekend with her boyfriend were correct.

The moment my daughter arrived home, I flew off the handle. I did not even give her a chance to say anything. I accused her of lying. I told her that I couldn't trust her, plus a lot of other awful and unkind statements that I was too outraged to remember. There was little or no communication after that. I was too angry to apologize for the manner in which I dealt with the situation, and she would not apologize for creating so much upset. The relationship deteriorated so badly that one day when I was away from the house, she packed her belongings and left.

My personal life was totally destroyed. Not eating and not sleeping were the norm each day. I felt as though I was just floating in air. Still angry, I wished she had not been born. I felt as if I was going through a bereavement period. The door to her room had to be closed because I couldn't stand to look inside. Thank god for my family and friends who were very supportive and understanding towards me.

SELF-DEFEATING THINKING

I kept thinking that I had failed. I remained angry and unforgiving. I thought that after all the effort I had made as a single parent, I deserved to be appreciated and not to be rejected and left in this state of mind.

NEW THINKING

After a few months, I started thinking that if she returned home, I would gladly take her back, but she never did and I had too much pride to ask her back. However, we established a line of communication and after a while I came to the realization that she was almost 20 years old and was going to live her life whatever way she chose. I wasn't doing anything with mine but destroying it. So gritting my teeth, I said to myself, "You better accept her and her way of life, otherwise she's lost forever."

EMOTIONAL RESPONSE

Having accepted the fact that she was now a woman living her own life, I decided to carry on with my life and let go of my daughter. I now felt better in myself that I had done the best I could for her, but I didn't relish the idea of our changed relationship.

SOLUTION AND OUTCOME

I started having a more active social life. I accepted that I did not control my daughter's life and that I must move on with mine. We communicated on an adult level and tried to respect one another's beliefs.

STICKING WITH IT

By accepting that my daughter is an adult and leaving home was her choice. It took a lot of effort on my part, but who said it was going to be easy.

SLIPPING BACK

I stop myself and say, "No, this doesn't work!"

ADVICE FOR OTHERS

Do not fly off the handle, listen, then act. Work out an understanding between you and your daughter or son. Seek professional help if necessary.

43: GETTING REMARRIED

Female, Age 38, Bookkeeper

ADVERSITY

I had been married for nine years. It was an unusual situation because we could live together quite nicely. He was my best friend and mentor; we were buddies. Although he was a good man, willing to give me everything I could possibly want materially, there was something missing in our lives. He was very much a person who could easily live on his own. His three loves were car racing, work, and me—in that order, so I was forced to live very much a separate life. He was unfaithful at one point, and from that time something happened to me. I could no longer have a sexual relationship with him. I couldn't stand to have him touch me. That part of me died, the chemistry was gone. I could be his friend, but not his lover, and strange as it may seem, I still really cared for him. We lived this way for four years where I couldn't give him the intimacy he needed. However, in time our relationship went down hill. We started to argue and fight. We could talk, but not about our deep feelings and what was lacking in the relationship. We were robbing ourselves of a meaningful life. Either I had to change how I felt about him sexually, which I couldn't, or I would have to leave. So I left. It was the most difficult step I'd ever taken.

I wasn't sure that I could manage on my own, I was afraid to go out alone, I didn't socialize much, and I was very lonely. I didn't want the "games," the stress, or the pressure of getting back into the dating scene. Emotionally I was simply petrified and strung out, just doing things yet not really being there.

My father and mother were of the old school—if you got married, it was for life and nothing less, no matter what. They didn't accept my reason to leave. According to them I should have stayed to work it out. So initially I had no support from them, although later, they came around. After I got remarried, they mellowed and were happy for me.

My work suffered badly when I was first on my own. I was a walking bag of emotions. If anything went wrong at the job, I would just come apart at the seams. I had trouble keeping my mind on what I was doing, yet I still managed to keep my job.

One crazy evening, I went on a blind date arranged by some very close friends. It was amazing that I allowed myself to go. One thing led to another and the relationship was suddenly becoming more intimate than I had anticipated. That's when I put on my brakes.

SELF-DEFEATING THINKING

I was afraid of my family's reaction because they were so fond of my previous husband. Also, I was scared to death of another relationship that might end up a repeat of my first marriage; on the other hand, I feared being alone. Overcome by uncertainty, doubt, and lack of confidence, I simply wasn't sure how far to go with this new man in my life. In the back of my mind, I knew that marriage would soon enter our conversation and this was taboo. I couldn't see myself in a permanent relationship again with the intense emotions and sexual closeness that came with it. How could I trust this man to be any different than my first husband? I kept wishing for someone to offer me the "right answer" so I could make a decision and get it over with.

NEW THINKING

When I stopped spinning my wheels, I realized that I could take care of myself and that this was the "right answer." If I permitted the relationship to develop further and found that the prospects of a second marriage were not for me, I would put a stop to it. It was then I acknowledged that I had allowed my independence, my self-confidence, and my decision-making ability to be robbed in my first marriage. My husband lost a lover and I lost myself. But this time around, I would not allow it to happen.

EMOTIONAL RESPONSE

I felt relieved that I could indeed see myself as a self-sufficient woman. I still felt cautious of this man's intentions and still a bit frightened. But I began to joke and laugh again, which was a positive step forward.

SOLUTION AND OUTCOME

I went out with this man quite regularly and allowed myself to enjoy each occasion. You need to appreciate that this went on for approximately two years. I needed to move at a speed that was comfortable for me. I got the space I needed from this man. He didn't force himself on me and he did not try to force me to commit to something I wasn't ready for. Not all men might be this patient, but he was, possibly because he knew that I would not tolerate an overbearing, overpowering approach.

STICKING WITH IT

I never think about it now. I have a husband and a child and a very full life. There's no reason for me to doubt myself as I previously did, because I have a wide circle of friends, which affords me a meaningful social life outside my marriage. I enjoy life within my marriage and have rewarding friendships outside my marriage.

SLIPPING BACK

All I have to do is think back on my previous marriage. This time when I see the communication between my husband and I slipping, I intervene almost immediately. I don't want a slippage in communication to become a major gap in our relationship. During my first marriage, we talked but never intimately understood one another. I make an effort to be more understanding, more attentive to my partner this time around. We may go out for a romantic, quiet dinner or simply spend time together in the den, with the T.V. shut off. In my first marriage, T.V. was a major part of our lifestyle.

ADVICE FOR OTHERS

Believe in yourself, try to learn to trust someone else again, because not everyone is the same. Tell yourself that you are worthwhile and can contribute to a worthwhile relationship.

44: HANDLING A TROUBLED TEENAGER

Male, Age 38, Chemist

ADVERSITY

We had a fast-paced lifestyle, my wife and I. Having four kids with both of us working made for a very busy schedule. There were a lot of arguments and disagreements at home, which were never resolved. Rather than communicate with the kids, we'd shout at them. If we didn't scream, my wife and I would not say too much because we lacked energy when we came home after a hectic day at work.

We were so caught up with what we were doing at work that our kids were often left on their own. One night my son got into a serious car accident and ended up in the hospital. From that point on, my son and I drifted apart even further. He only stayed in the hospital overnight for observation, but after he arrived home, our contact with one another was minimal. We didn't say much when we were together, which kept me wondering what was wrong with my teenage son.

During my quiet times at home, which were more frequent lately, I'd reflect and ask myself what had happened to the relationship between my son and me. I knew I was to blame and felt very guilty about it. I had simply let things slide and my son had done the same. But I should know better. After all, I was supposed to be his father who could offer him guidance, support, care, and attention. None of this was happening and I knew that it was hurting him. I heard from neighbors that my son was more aloof, less talkative, less involved at school, and generally not the same. Yet we kept avoiding one another at home, as if a permanent barrier had been erected never to be taken down.

The predicament put me in a very embarrassing position. I found it awkward around my friends, especially when I'd be asked about the kids. As for my parents and in-laws, they had some sense about what was going on and were prepared to offer what help they could. I was very heartened to see all of us pull together in an attempt to see what could be done for my son.

My colleagues at work told me that I was not myself lately. They noticed that I was crankier, more tense, more irritable, and simply "not there."

SELF-DEFEATING THINKING

I kept thinking of what had happened between us and kept on blaming my busy schedule and myself for putting off my plans to talk to my son who now seemed alienated from me. Somehow I had sensed before that something was wrong, but I never acted on it as I should have. I was a lousy father.

NEW THINKING

I told myself that our relationship had seriously deteriorated and that I needed to do something about it right away. If I procrastinated as before, I might make matters considerably worse. Sooner or later I would need to face it, so do it now. It's hard for a parent to admit failure and to accept blame, but that's what has to happen sometimes, before action takes place.

EMOTIONAL RESPONSE

I felt nervous for fear that my son would reject my sincere overtures. I really wanted to get to know him and find out what had gone wrong between us. Was it too late, was a question I kept asking myself.

SOLUTION AND OUTCOME

Pulling myself together, I approached my son with the offering that I wanted to have a heart-to-heart talk with him. He immediately rejected the idea and declared that it was too late for that. Shock was registered all over me. My worst fears had come true. But interestingly, I didn't stop there because I was more determined than ever before.

STICKING WITH IT

I proceeded to write my son a lengthy letter describing what had happened to me and how I had let myself and him down. Also, I pointed out my deepest concern for him and his troubles. A solution was proposed that initially involved an open discussion, with a time and date put forth. I did have a meeting with my son, although the results at first were not that promising. However, I've been able to continue talking with him and that's what keeps me going.

SLIPPING BACK

I tell myself that I will not repeat the same mistakes. My family is too important. That is not to say that my work isn't, but quantity and quality of time with family needs to be part of every week.

ADVICE FOR OTHERS

Admit that you as a parent are by no means perfect. Secondly, admit that your children can have problems that in part, may be due to your failure to understand them and to support them. Dinner time can be an opportunity for all to exchange ideas, whereas individual conferences can be set up to share more intimate details. Plan more time together outside of the home. Communicate by writing notes and stick them on a bulletin board or the fridge door. Express love by hugging, touching, and make jokes once in a while to create a more relaxed atmosphere.

45: PREMATURE BIRTH

Female, Age 41, Homemaker

ADVERSITY

After a very hectic day of shopping, running around, and more shopping, I finally got home late at night and flopped into bed. The next day, I was having coffee with my neighbors in the kitchen and felt this big gush. I thought I was wetting my pants. I was so embarrassed that I didn't say anything. I waited until they left and then said to my husband that something was wrong because I was soaking wet. We didn't think much of it, but I really didn't know if I was voiding or if my water broke. I let it go on until midnight and then finally called my doctor.

When I phoned her, she said I better get to the hospital right away because I was still six weeks early. I went to the hospital and had a stress test and physical examination. Although my water had broken, I wasn't ready to deliver, but I was told to stay in the hospital. After about two weeks that seemed like two months, I went into labor.

My husband had to get his mother to stay at our house, because we had another child at home who was only four years old. My husband had to take care of our child, do the laundry, and do the cooking. Although he had help from his mother, it was hard for them because they were so worried. I had a hard time getting pregnant with this baby. We had gone for fertility studies and went through a considerable ordeal until I got pregnant, and all of a sudden to go in the hospital, weeks before I was due, was very scary. And not knowing if it was going to turn out well or not was even more disturbing.

I remembered that during my stay not too many friends came to see me. Were they worried about coming to see me and not knowing what to say? Many people aren't too sure what to say in a bad situation.

My co-workers were surprised to hear that I was in the hospital, but many came to visit. They were all very supportive. Also, because of my long stay, I became quite friendly with the obstetrics nurses who would keep me busy by giving me books to read, paper and pencil games, and so on.

SELF-DEFEATING THINKING

I thought a lot about the possibility of the baby dying and what I would do and how I'd react. At times I got worried because the baby wasn't moving enough. I was having a fetal stress test every day. It seemed like there was more activity during some days than others. They were checking my vital signs often and checked the fetal heart rate regularly. Sometimes the fetal heart rate was very low, sometimes it was high. I just didn't know what was going to happen and this terrified me. Never before had I been in such a position of not knowing, and this really got to me.

NEW THINKING

I convinced myself that this was not my fault. With my first pregnancy, I worked until the last week before delivery and everything went well. Now I was no longer working but resting carefully in hospital and following medical instructions. I convinced myself that it didn't matter what I thought because whatever happened, would happen, despite my worry and fears. There was nothing I could do at this point.

EMOTIONAL RESPONSE

I still didn't feel any better, but I just tolerated it more. It seemed that there was a 50/50 chance of success. I was constantly losing amniotic fluid and worried about how long I could keep losing this fluid without the baby being harmed or injured.

SOLUTION AND OUTCOME

Once I decided that there wasn't much I could do to change the situation, I just went along with it and tried to think positively.

STICKING WITH IT

I just refused to think negatively and pessimistically. I took up my time with reading and knitting to keep my mind off my problem while in the hospital.

Luckily my child was alright when he was born. Two years later I was pregnant again and went through the same situation, but this time with less fear and worry. Again the chances of a successful birth were 50/50. This one worked out as well.

SLIPPING BACK

When I start worrying, I talk myself out of it. There is no point to worrying about something I have no control over.

ADVICE FOR OTHERS

Don't take this matter lightly like I did at first, but also do not worry yourself to death. Adopt a realistic and positive attitude and follow medical instructions carefully. Finally, don't leave your husband out, be certain to include him.

46: POVERTY

Male, Age 68, Minister

ADVERSITY

I had been brought up in a very poor family with five other brothers and sisters, and at times only had bread and water. My family was very stable and resourceful and, although times were tough, we always managed to get by using the barter system.

I finally became a Salvation Army officer and went to my first posting in a very remote community in the northwest part of the country, without any money, expecting the person in charge to at least have some food. Eventually I found the house in which I was to reside. Much to my dismay, I found a pile of old dirty clothes covered with a sheet. Presumably this was a bed and there was not a thing to eat.

I was filled with despair and didn't know what to do. At this point I was very tempted to quit. My self-respect and honor did not allow me to speak ill of the individual who invited me to this house, but my opinion of this person certainly changed.

SELF-DEFEATING THINKING

Was this to be my calling? Why was I brought to this poverty-stricken existence? Was it not enough to be brought up under these conditions, without having to now do my work under these same circumstances?

NEW THINKING

I remember that I had a personal relationship with God and decided to completely trust in whatever he had in store for me. I turned to prayer and my instruction was to go and knock on the first door I came to and I would find help. I did this and the woman who answered the door listened to my request for help and responded without hesitation. She later became the matron of honor for my fiancee when we were married.

EMOTIONAL RESPONSE

I had total faith in my prayers and in the instructions that I had received.

SOLUTION AND OUTCOME

The woman I spoke to at the door essentially adopted me as her own son and being part of her family eliminated my problem of poverty.

STICKING WITH IT

Because of my past frugal existence, living in poor surroundings was not a tremendous burden. However, after marriage my wife and I decided that we wanted to have a reasonably comfortable retirement, which our pensions would not provide for us. So I found a job in a funeral home and within five years reached our financial goal. I retired and we began to enjoy our winters down south and resided in a nice apartment during the summer months up north among friends and relatives.

SLIPPING BACK

My faith is so strong that I always rely on God to fulfill my needs, and I have yet to be disappointed.

ADVICE FOR OTHERS

People must have the motivation first to make a change in their lives and no one can give this to them. Determination to overcome the stumbling blocks that have contributed to poverty needs to come from within. Once that internal spark is there, make it eternal!

47: UNWANTED PREGNANCY IN THE FAMILY

Female, Age 62, Nursery School Teacher

ADVERSITY

Early last year my unmarried daughter, age 38, hinted that she would like to have a baby. She said that she didn't want to get married, but wanted to have a child. My daughter often talked about her married friends and their family problems, and her separated or divorced friends and their custody problems. I thought that she was just trying to get a reaction, to shock me, so I didn't pay much attention at the time. That was the first and last opportunity we had to discuss it. My daughter has lived independently for many years, and she owns a condominium apartment.

One late summer evening, my daughter and I were sitting at the dining room table, when she asked, "How would you feel about becoming a grandma?" I thought that she was referring to my son and his wife, who had been married a few months ago, and replied that they both seemed very career-oriented at the present time. Then she explained that she, herself, was pregnant. She had just been to see a doctor to confirm her pregnancy, which was very much planned, not accidental. Apparently she had been holding down a second job to prepare financially.

First, I wondered how I would tell my husband who is old-world European. Then how would other relatives and friends react once told about this unusual prospect. After her announcement to me, my daughter kept pressuring me to speak to my husband (her father) and tell him the "wonderful news." But I couldn't immediately. I needed time to think and to gauge his reaction as well as the reaction of others.

SELF-DEFEATING THINKING

My friends would think that I was an inept mother for raising a daughter who would do something like this. They would be so disgusted that I might lose some of them as friends. My relatives would be shocked with disgust and my husband would deplore this mess and might even disown her. This was such a worry and tension filled time for me.

NEW THINKING

There's nothing I can do about this. It's done and I have no control over the outcome. My daughter, I thought, was healthy, mature, financially independent, and emotionally stable. There was less stigma attached to being an unwed mother in today's society with its multitude of family configurations. I finally realized that I was looking at this as if it had taken place 20 years ago when society was far less tolerant of different lifestyles.

EMOTIONAL RESPONSE

I became more concerned about the practical aspects of helping my daughter prepare for the new baby rather than worrying about what everyone might say.

SOLUTION AND OUTCOME

I became preoccupied with my daughter's physical health, her long working schedule, her diet, her exercise, and her general state of well-being. The important thing now was for her to remain as healthy as possible. By the way, my friends reacted most favorably when I told them, and my husband surprisingly became very protective and felt that our daughter should see a lawyer to assure that the natural father couldn't get custody of the child.

STICKING WITH IT

Sometimes I worried about the future and what might happen, but I was primarily concerned about the present and being most helpful to my daughter.

SLIPPING BACK

Activity seems to be the answer. Also, I tell myself to "shape up!"—and then I get busy knitting and sewing for the baby.

ADVICE FOR OTHERS

My advice is to be as supportive as possible.

48: SERIOUS FINANCIAL PROBLEMS

Male, Age 29, Subcontractor

ADVERSITY

I was getting set up in my own business, which involved buying tools, a truck, and other necessary equipment. There was also a tax transition involved, where I was responsible for controlling my tax payments to the government, versus payroll tax deductions.

Overwhelmed with the amount of cash at my disposal, I spent large amounts of money on personal enjoyment rather than concentrating on loan and tax payments.

Having a great time and being extravagant were top priority. On the other hand, life at home became stressful due to numerous arguments with my girlfriend over loan payments and daily living expenses. She thought I was being too irresponsible and she was probably correct. But nothing really mattered except hard work Monday to Friday and my active social life during the weekend where spending what I earned was the objective. It got so bad that I wasn't able to cover my business expense payments. Threatening letters were being sent to my apartment about having my tools and my truck confiscated. I was afraid to open the mail for fear of what I'd find. It seemed like I was on a course of financial self-destruction, yet it didn't seem to matter. I had a lot of money and was determined to spend it and show others how I could enjoy it.

SELF-DEFEATING THINKING

Nothing terrible would happen to me. I just had to make more money, then I'd get the debts off my back. Why shouldn't I enjoy myself, I deserved it. After all I'd worked so hard during the weekdays, I had to make up for it on the weekends. The best part was showing my friends what kind of a sport I was. I liked being a "big shot" and throwing money around both on myself and on my buddies.

NEW THINKING

My problem came to a crisis when the slow winter season arrived and little money was coming in. I finally realized that I might lose everything. The business that I had developed was in serious jeopardy. Why was I so stupid as to deny my problem for so long? For the first time I accepted that I was the problem.

EMOTIONAL RESPONSE

I felt very upset, nervous, and panic-ridden. But this didn't stop me from planning a course of action. It's interesting how when you reach bottom, suddenly everything becomes very clear. I knew I had a lot of potential and that I better start living up to it.

SOLUTION AND OUTCOME

I came to understand what the real problem was. My socializing included travelling around with a crowd where cocaine use was abundant. I personally came to terms with my cocaine problem and with the help of some very close friends began to slowly get off the stuff. Also, I got rid of my apartment and moved to another part of town with the hope of abandoning my old drug buddies. At times like this, you also find out who really cares for you. Some fellow contractors got together and helped me to get my finances under control.

STICKING WITH IT

Feeling better and healthier about myself allowed me to change my priorities. I was able to meet all of my financial commitments and began to manage my finances more wisely.

SLIPPING BACK

I continued to use cocaine occasionally, and felt guilty and angry with myself after each episode. I realized the potential for financial disaster, which I did not wish to repeat. At the same time I recognized that I couldn't quit on my own because I was addicted. So I admitted myself into treatment. This was the best step I'd ever taken.

ADVICE FOR OTHERS

I would advise others with this problem not to be afraid to admit your short-comings and seek help before your situation is so out of control and you can

113

no longer rectify it. I have known some people who went bankrupt and lost everything just for the sake of a cocaine addiction!

49: RAISING A DISABLED CHILD

Female, Age 38, Homemaker

ADVERSITY

With one healthy five-year-old child, our second baby was eagerly awaited. My joy in hearing our baby's first cry was dampened by my doctor's voice saying, "It's just too bad." He thought I was still unconscious. The baby was immaturely developed. He had an extra finger, and worst of all he had an ugly facial deformity that included a large hair lip and total cleft palate.

I was unable to cope and wanted to go away and hide. I didn't want to talk with my husband or play with my older daughter. Depression and many crying spells took up part of the day, while dragging myself to complete household chores and listening to the radio took up the other part of the day.

My older child became less playful and tended to spend more time with her father. Friends talked to me on the phone or came to offer their best wishes, but I still felt that I was alone in my misery.

I dropped out of my church volunteer group. It took all of my energy to prepare for baby's return from hospital.

SELF-DEFEATING THINKING

Why me? Is God trying to punish me for some reason? I heard that birth defects were inherited. Would our grandchildren be like this too? Would they find more things wrong with our baby? Would he be like a neighborhood girl, whom I remember as a child being retarded and tormented by the other kids? How could I manage him? I didn't have experience in caring for such a helpless baby! What if he died and it was my fault?

NEW THINKING

One day I couldn't keep my fears to myself and I told my husband. He just said, "Don't worry. We'll just do the best we can. That's all we can do. The baby didn't ask to be born. It is our duty to care for him. If you treat him like a 'normal child,' he will turn out okay." We started making plans to hire help in the house, as I spent one hour out of every three in round-the-clock feeding because he couldn't swallow properly.

We sold some bonds to pay for plastic surgery. I started to think constructively again. With help from my husband and friends, I did my best to keep going. Everyone was on our side. The doctors were depending on me too. I would do it. I had to.

EMOTIONAL RESPONSE

Tired all of the time—"jet lag" for one year. As the days went on, the feelings of hopelessness began to disappear.

SOLUTION AND OUTCOME

I didn't have much time to worry. We were able to lead a normal life after the surgery. The baby had survived thanks to me the doctor said. He learned to talk and we took him out in public. I felt more confident about his future.

STICKING WITH IT

Everything came together slowly. I still worried about the grandchildren inheriting deformities. My son did well after surgery. He looked okay and he was smart in school.

SLIPPING BACK

I tell myself, "Nothing turns out as bad as it seems at the time." You just have to organize your priorities, put your energies and abilities to good use, and forget about what might happen. Quit worrying and do your best job.

ADVICE FOR OTHERS

My cousin had a cleft palate child. I told her to give the baby all the love you can. Don't be afraid to express your innermost fears. It's normal. Nowadays surgeons can indeed work "miracles," as they did with my son.

Anyone who has a deformed baby can create their own miracle. It's no use worrying and getting depressed. Rally together all the help you can get. Be prepared to be exhausted for a time. Finally, believe that things will work out!

50: LOSS OF A PARENT

Female, Age 36, Senior Nurse

ADVERSITY

My father, to whom I was very close, died at the hospital on the same floor where I was working. He was diagnosed as having lung cancer and was admitted to oncology, where he was treated and passed away six months later. It was emotionally difficult, at times impossible, for me to first cope with my father's illness. Family members would ask me many questions and would depend on me for answers because I was a nurse. It was difficult to go to work and give the patients under my care the physical and emotional support a good oncology nurse should give. Each day I had to ask God for strength to cope.

When my father passed away, I took four days from work and then returned, as my mother felt that since she did, so I should. What everyone didn't realize was that I was returning to where it happened. It was devastating. I had no strength to provide support to my patients and couldn't handle caring for cancer patients, especially people with lung cancer.

My personal life changed in that my base, my foundation that had stood by me throughout my childhood and adult life had crumbled. I could always count on my parents, especially my dad. His children were everything to him.

My husband's mother died 16 years ago of lung cancer so he understood what I was going through.

My problem occurred with my mother. She felt that she had lost her husband, I still had mine, so why couldn't I function at work. Our relationship became quite strained. Speaking freely to her was unacceptable because she would get too upset, yet my dad always encouraged me to be open and honest. To express my disappointment at her lack of empathy was feedback she was not prepared to tolerate. How could she not understand that he was the only father I would ever have? I was mourning too!

My working relationships were surprisingly unchanged and a great comfort to me. Everyone had known my dad and felt a close bond to me and my family. Oncology nursing is very special. It takes a special person to do it well. When I returned to work, it was suggested that I look after the surgical patients on the floor. Unfortunately, most of the surgery patients were having operations because of cancer. It was inevitable I would be called upon to wipe tears, comfort a wife or son, after bad news.

SELF-DEFEATING THINKING

After each work shift, I would go home and cry, vowing never to return. I hated it and the way my life had turned out. The real concern I grew to realize was that I was alone for the first time in my life. My base of support had fallen. I had lost a parent; I didn't feel like a whole person. Each day at work was a constant reminder to me of my loss and my longing for my dad whom I loved with all my heart and soul. Next to my husband, he was my dearest friend and confidant. Would I run away and hide or would I stay and fight my feelings? This dilemma haunted me daily.

NEW THINKING

After almost six weeks, one day I decided I had to do something for my sake, and my husband's too. My father would not want to see me suffering because of him. He would have been upset with me. This thinking began to help me. I used his love in a different way, to give me strength and courage. That day I spoke with a close friend who was also a colleague. Through open discussion, and openly thinking about myself and my goals, and also using my dad's strength, I was able for the first time to admit my loss and to try to deal with it and not run away.

EMOTIONAL RESPONSE

I felt better, not 100 percent, but improving. I felt less hopeless. Before I had felt like I had no options. I think in a crisis situation, a person only sees the bad, the negative. In grieving, I couldn't see or separate my emotions from anything else.

SOLUTION AND OUTCOME

Dying is a part of life that each person must face eventually. I became a nurse because it was something I had always wanted to do and my father was very proud of me on graduation day. He had done a good job raising his children and he could die knowing that. His family life was fulfilling and he was a happy man when he passed away. Knowing this now, I left oncology and accepted a position in obstetrics and family practice. The change was very good for me, and I can honestly say I enjoy my work. There isn't a day that goes by that I don't think of my father, but I don't feel overwhelmed as I once did.

STICKING WITH IT

I know that my dad would not have wanted me to be so upset. The day he died, I cried all over his face and I caught myself saying, "Daddy, you'd be upset because I'm crying so much." I've always been a strong person, and this life experience was the weakest and lowest point in my life. It's difficult to see yourself this way, wondering if you'll ever feel the same again. After the initial grieving process for whatever length of time, and after I changed jobs, things seemed to fall into place.

SLIPPING BACK

This is difficult to answer. If I encounter a patient with cancer, I still find it hard to offer emotional support. I see my father in this patient, remembering what he went through. But I allow myself to go through the thinking process now, which I would not have let myself do before. I'm able to get through the difficult moments and function, whereas before I would have cried and not been able to continue.

ADVICE FOR OTHERS

Mine was an unusual situation. In speaking to many nurses, I discovered none who had had a relative die in the same hospital on the same floor where they worked.

No one can slow down or speed up the grieving process. All family and friends can do is listen and be there for support. Use the individuals who want to help. Also, know that a lot of grieving must be done alone. Know that it does get better, you always miss your loved one, but one day the pain is replaced with wonderful memories of happy times. Allow yourself to cry, be angry, and so forth. If speaking to outsiders helps, do it. There is no shame in seeking help. No one can ever bring my dad back, but no one will ever erase from my heart and mind the thoughts of the best dad anyone ever had!!

51: PRESSURED INTO MARRIAGE

Female, Age 23, Secretary/Typist

ADVERSITY

Due to lack of communication and other factors, I was having increasing arguments with my spouse. As a result, I felt very frustrated and hurt, both at him and at my family.

I met my husband when I was 13 years old. I grew to like him, and we started dating. My parents found out that I was dating him, so they forced me to marry him (it was our culture not to date before marriage) at the age of 18. He was 21 at the time and was already living on his own with a steady job. He was more mature than I was and wanted desperately to get married. Everybody in the family wanted me to agree to the offer of matrimony.

Getting married early, especially when I wasn't ready for it, backfired. I was very depressed because my adolescent life was over. As I kept thinking about school, and all the things that I was missing, the crying increased. I tried to make the best of living with my husband, but we never got along. He prevented me from seeing my parents whom I missed very much. They were upset and I was upset with my husband, but there was nothing that could be done.

There was never time to go out with my friends because my husband wanted me at home, so I lost contact with them. My salvation was my job, which I got about one month after we married. There I could get engrossed in what I was doing and literally forget about my life at home.

SELF-DEFEATING THINKING

The first couple of months I accepted the marriage and tried to make the best of it, but it seemed that all my husband wanted was somebody to cook and care for him. He didn't love me, and I knew it. Yet the arguments continued to increase and it got so bad that he would hit me. He struck me on a number of occasions when he became bossy and lost control. Sometimes we tried to talk about the problems, but it got nowhere, so I ignored him and the problems.

119

I was so indecisive and unsure of myself that I was lost about what to do. My life was in a complete mess and whom did I blame but my parents for forcing this decision on me to marry him. My parents were even concerned that we were fighting, repeatedly telling me to stay devoted to my husband and the marriage. I allowed myself to think that I should stay in the relationship for my parents. After all, if I left the marriage, it would destroy them and the rest of the family.

NEW THINKING

At first we tried to solve our problems, but nothing would ever work out. He would come home from work and just watch television. We talked a few times, and things would be fine for about a week, then everything returned to the way it was. This continued and I reached a point where I told myself that I didn't want this man for my husband or this relationship for my marriage. I simply refused to stand for this any longer, even at the risk of being beaten. I refused to waste any more of my life on a man whom I did not love.

EMOTIONAL RESPONSE

I was scared because I didn't know if I was making the right decision, and I wasn't sure of what I really wanted. Never had I really made decisions, as my parents had always made them for me. Afraid or not, it had to be done.

SOLUTION AND OUTCOME

One rainy evening, I walked into the den and told him I was leaving. He didn't care if I left and didn't even raise his hand to me. I left him and never looked back. Staying with my two sisters who loved me helped to ease the transition. My regret is that I allowed my parents, especially my mother, to force me into marrying him. Although precious time in my life was wasted, I was determined not to repeat this ever again.

STICKING WITH IT

I feel better now, and I prefer this way of living. When I think about the marriage, it still hurts; but I am young and I am able to start over and resume a meaningful and happy life. Also, the support that I receive from my sisters and friends is very important to me and has taken me through some tough times.

SLIPPING BACK

Now I won't let anybody tell me what to do. I make decisions and stick by them. Although my parents still try to pressure me into doing things their way, I challenge them and return to my own decisions. My maturity and independence have certainly grown.

ADVICE FOR OTHERS

My advice to someone else would be to think very carefully about what you are doing, especially if you are considering marriage at a young age. And whatever you do, don't allow yourself to be pressured into a decision you will regret later. Marriage is an important bond not to be taken lightly but very seriously.

52: INCONSIDERATE NEIGHBOR

Female, Age 44, Store Owner

ADVERSITY

New neighbors moved in next door with a cute dog called Snoopy. Snoopy was allowed to run free every morning and evening and you can imagine where he went to the bathroom! Right! On my lawn.

I hated this animal defecating on my property, especially since I had to clean it up. Every time I saw this animal in my yard I would fume because I knew I would be the one scooping up the crap. The neighbors were so inconsiderate, allowing this mutt to roam around unattended.

At first I scooped the poop and put it on their patio, but they didn't notice. Then I put it on their front walk and that didn't make a difference. A friend suggested that I put it in their mailbox, but I resisted. As you could see, the relationship with these neighbors was strained to say the least, and I was afraid to say anything to them.

SELF-DEFEATING THINKING

I thought about the dog on the lawn and how insensitive and inconsiderate these neighbors really were. How could they allow their dog to run loose and not be responsible enough to control its actions? I kept rehearsing in my mind what I should say to these people. But I guess what held me back was concern about their reaction. Would they get upset with me? Would I be able to handle their reaction?

NEW THINKING

I knew I had to do something. I couldn't live with myself if I didn't say something to them. If they got mad, then I'd deal with it as best I could. But I couldn't allow this to go on while I sat in my house and stewed about it.

EMOTIONAL RESPONSE

I felt good that I had made a decision to say something, but was still somewhat concerned about their reaction.

SOLUTION AND OUTCOME

One morning on the weekend, I took a deep breath and went next door. I told them quite simply that I was upset with their dog running loose and also bothered about this animal pooping on my lawn. They were reasonable about it and said that they would try to keep Snoopy off my property.

STICKING WITH IT

The dog did not come by as often, but would still drop an occasional poop on my lawn. So I put up a cedar hedge and this seemed to block the dog's path to my property.

SLIPPING BACK

I tell myself to express my concerns and not let them bother me so much. Why should I worry about such trivial matters? Instead I should address them quickly.

ADVICE FOR OTHERS

Confronting the issue directly solves a lot of problems. If you address issues early, they will remain small and solvable; otherwise, you may be unnecessarily aggravated.

53: DEATH OF A CHILD

Female, Age 38, Occupational Therapist

ADVERSITY

After 17 weeks of being pregnant, an ultrasound revealed that my fetus had a bladder abnormality, possibly Potter's syndrome. If the pregnancy continued, the baby would die shortly after birth. There was no hope for surgical repair at birth. My options were to abort the fetus or to complete the pregnancy. My religious and personal beliefs influenced my decision to go ahead with the pregnancy. My husband and two children were most supportive of my decision.

After my decision I became very depressed. I didn't want to socialize with people, and I missed a number of social events including an important wedding. I literally remained home during the pregnancy, because facing friends and relatives was too difficult.

At work I was constantly distracted by thoughts of the baby and what might have gone wrong.

SELF-DEFEATING THINKING

What did I do to cause this to happen? I recounted everything about the pregnancy and carefully considered what food I had eaten, my lifestyle, and the working environment. Even though the industrial hygienist at work checked my video display terminal, I thought about that too. What went wrong?

I also kept wondering if my choice to go through with the pregnancy was allowing the baby to suffer.

NEW THINKING

I prayed a lot and counted my blessings, because I had a lot to be grateful for. A husband, two healthy children, and good personal health were my salvations. I thanked God for giving me the time to prepare for what was to happen. My problem, I reminded myself, was still not as bad as the misfortunes others had to face.

I decided to make the best of it and treated the pregnancy like a normal one. I ate well, took care of myself, and did everything I could in the best interest of the baby. Although at times I was really upset, I refused the Valium that the doctor offered me.

I decided to find out more about what went wrong. The genetic counselling that I received indicated that the odds were one in a million it would happen again. The research that I read in the medical library also was quite informative.

We decided as a family that the baby should have an identity. This included giving it a name, and having a funeral to say goodbye when the time came. We also had a picture taken just after the baby died, so we could remember this member of the family.

My family and I believed God had a purpose in this. Maybe the baby and we were being spared a permanent severe handicap it would sustain, destroying its quality of life.

After the baby was born, he lived for 1½ hours. I held him and talked to him until he died. We had the funeral. I never saw my husband cry as he did. Although we were very upset, I counted my blessings and appreciated what I had.

How grateful I was to God for giving me the strength to go through the nine months. Also, I was thankful for the short and easy two-hour labor.

EMOTIONAL RESPONSE

I felt much better. I did what I could do. I have no regrets about how things went. Although I still get sad at times, it is getting easier.

SOLUTION AND OUTCOME

My relationships with my family and friends became closer. My husband and I have discussed having another baby, and I think we will.

STICKING WITH IT

God's strength. Setting goals for the future, like that of having another baby, and looking after my family and my home life are important. Because I have no regrets, it helps to keep me going. I cherish the memory of him, and the knowledge that he is in heaven. I still talk a lot about it with my husband and children.

SLIPPING BACK

I remember I did all I could, and I have no regrets. I have faith that it was in God's plan. I count my blessings, and I talk about it with my family and friends.

Weigh your blessings. Analyze what you have in comparison to others. Talk about it with your close friends and family. Also, pray a lot.

54: GAMBLING PROBLEM IN THE FAMILY

Male, Age 28, Assembly Line Worker

ADVERSITY

I had been working at the factory for years and was bored. The guys I hung out with really enjoyed going to the track, so I joined them almost every day. Being single and unattached meant I didn't have many responsibilities, so why not gamble and make some quick, easy money.

I lived with a friend who was always telling me to quit betting on horses because it was a waste of money. But I was used to living from paycheck to paycheck and being broke. Sooner or later I'd get lucky and get a big win and make up what I'd lost and more.

My parents, although inquisitive, didn't really know what I was up to and I wouldn't have told them anyways. None of my family had ever gambled away their money, and I wasn't going to let them know that I was the first.

SELF-DEFEATING THINKING

I kept thinking one of these days I'm going to win big. It was an addiction. The more I believed I was going to win, the harder it became to keep away from the track.

NEW THINKING

I started paying attention to the people who went to the track. Some were bums. Many were alone . . . what kind of life did they have? Was I going to become a lonely bum? I wasn't going anywhere except broke. And fast.

I had to be better than this! If I didn't get my act together, my future would be lost.

EMOTIONAL RESPONSE

I felt like a jerk. I felt so stupid that I had lost thousands of dollars.

SOLUTION AND OUTCOME

Just as I was hoping to get my life back together again, I met someone whom I eventually married. Now there was something to look forward to. My priorities changed. I just stopped going to the track cold turkey.

STICKING WITH IT

I have a family now, I can't just throw away money by gambling. Why jeopardize my happy life? Also, getting rid of my horse-betting buddies has made it easier for me.

SLIPPING BACK

Gambling on horses or anything else is like throwing or giving your money away. You simply cannot get ahead. There are better things to do with your hard-earned dollars.

ADVICE FOR OTHERS

Get help from an organization that is set up to assist gamblers. Try to think of someone who has become rich gambling and you'll come up with the same answer I did—none. Most gamblers are in debt. Stay close to friends and family for support; I didn't and probably should have.

55: INABILITY TO HAVE CHILDREN

Female, Age 36, Chiropractor

ADVERSITY

After five years of trying to conceive, without success, I realized that we needed medical advice. My husband and I were referred to a specialist. For the next two years, I went through every test and took every pill ever marketed for infertility. The result was still no pregnancy. Although frustrated, I still persisted.

The hardest part of trying to conceive was that lovemaking became very mechanical; we tried only on certain days at certain times, all the spontaneity was gone.

My profession kept me busy and basically I buried myself in my work to take my mind off what was happening to me personally. The only time things were awkward was when a member of the staff became pregnant. They would be afraid to tell me. Although I was truly happy for my peers, it always reminded me of my problem. Although I wouldn't noticeably show my pain as I learned of their good news, I did go home and shed a few tears.

SELF-DEFEATING THINKING

The only medical problem that the specialist found was my husband's low sperm count. However, they felt we could still very well conceive. So under medical direction we tried and tried. I guess I just kept asking myself, "Why? Why me?"—but I never came up with an answer.

NEW THINKING

I finally accepted the fact that there was a very real possibility that I would not have my own child. Too many years of unsuccessful trying had worn us out. It was time to accept our fate and get on with life.

EMOTIONAL RESPONSE

I did not like what fate had dished out, but that was the way it was and I had to accept it.

SOLUTION AND OUTCOME

We applied to adopt a child and hoped that all would work out for us. I ceased thinking every month that I might get pregnant.

STICKING WITH IT

By accepting the fact that no matter what life throws at me, I have the resilience to cope. This perspective has allowed me to deal with other major hardships.

SLIPPING BACK

I tell myself that fate dealt me a hard blow, but life still goes on.

ADVICE FOR OTHERS

Try all the medical routes first and then apply for adoption. I am very proud to say that we were fortunate enough to adopt the most beautiful girl in the world, who has brought us more joy than I could have ever imagined.

56: SALE OF A HOME

Female, Age 29, Hairdresser

ADVERSITY

We were having some problems with the neighbors who expected our three boys not to make any noise. Because our backyards were small and close to one another, it made for many disagreements. I didn't want to leave the neighborhood because I was very comfortable and had many friends on the street. On the other hand, my husband was fed up with the neighbors and also wanted the children to have a decent size backyard to play in. I was worried about where we would go, how much we would have to pay for another home, and how much we would get for our place.

SELF-DEFEATING THINKING

I really didn't know what to do. Never before had I been so indecisive and I hated it. I didn't want to leave the neighborhood, yet I knew that we should get away, for our sake and our kids. Every night my husband read the ads in the paper to me and every evening I got more anxious and confused. He didn't seem to care where we moved as long as we got away.

NEW THINKING

I told myself to stop stewing and worrying and that I needed to make a decision and stick to it. The most important thing, I told myself, was to stop being afraid of change. Being brought up to value security and stability made it difficult adjusting to different situations. Now was the time to take hold of myself and do what was best for our family.

EMOTIONAL RESPONSE

I was filled with conviction. Change will always surround me so learning to handle it was important.

SOLUTION AND OUTCOME

We put a for sale sign on our front lawn. My husband and I discussed what price we were prepared to accept and what we were willing to pay for another house.

STICKING WITH IT

I realize that I can make another comfortable home for myself in another neighborhood. There is no reason for me to lose contact with my old neighbors. I'll stay in touch, yet it is important to separate myself and look forward to new people and new relationships. In the past I would have been terrified of this kind of change.

SLIPPING BACK

I remind myself about how happy my husband will be and how excited my boys will be to get away from our cranky neighbors and to move into a house with a big yard.

_____

Try and work out all of your concerns with your spouse first, before deciding upon the move. Also remind yourself that change in and of itself is worthwhile and enriching. When we allow ourselves to get trapped by our possessions, we miss out on life!

57: SEXUAL PROBLEMS IN THE MARRIAGE

Female, Age 52, Dietitian

ADVERSITY _____

I was unable to have sexual intercourse due to my husband's inability to have and maintain penile erection, resulting from health problems and renal transplant surgery. Each day I would contend with his anger, frustration, and depression—and his declining self-esteem. He prided himself on being somewhat of a macho man and his impotence was a sign to him that he had lost his virility. As he grew more irritable, I became more tense—and both of us took out our moods on our two adolescent sons. Although I was not overly upset about not having intercourse because I was often tired from a busy job and from caring for a convalescent husband, I was worried about our argumentative relationship.

SELF-DEFEATING THINKING _____

I thought how pathetic my husband seemed. Yet I was bothered by his moods. He didn't have the right to take his frustrations out on our sons and myself. Our family and friends even noticed his change of personality. Both of us made a point of avoiding any discussion about the issue with others. In essence I was alone with this problem.

NEW THINKING _____

I constantly reminded myself that things could be a lot worse. Besides, we hadn't yet received proper professional help to deal with his impotence.

EMOTIONAL RESPONSE

Hopeful yet realistic is the best way to describe it. I knew that it would be a struggle for my husband to feel sexually capable again.

SOLUTION AND OUTCOME

We were referred to a clinic where my husband received drug injections, which unfortunately were not successful. However, with professional counselling and therapy, my husband and I were able to explore and experiment with alternative lovemaking techniques that have been satisfying to both of us.

STICKING WITH IT

My sexual relationship with my husband has improved vastly and he has been able to satisfy me sexually without actual intercourse. Because both of us have tried to satisfy each other using alternative methods, our lovemaking has increased in regularity.

SLIPPING BACK

Both of us have found our current sexual relationship very satisfying. We have come to the realization that there are other ways or techniques to please and satisfy each other's needs.

ADVICE FOR OTHERS

First of all, maintain a good sense of humor as it will certainly help you through the tough times. Mostly it is important to experiment and to be creative when making love. There are many other ways to satisfy one another sexually, and not have to rely on intercourse. Finally, seek out professional counselling. It was the critical factor in overcoming our difficulties.

58: DISCIPLINARY PROBLEMS WITH CHILD

Female, Age 32, Career Consultant

ADVERSITY

I started noticing disciplinary problems with my son when he was six months old. He started pulling people's hair and it took up to one year to stop him from doing it. When he became three years old, we couldn't take him shopping because he wouldn't sit still in the buggy. He was hyperactive, defiant, and very aggressive, especially towards his sister.

Our family began to visit less frequently, because when he played with their children he became too uncontrollable and wild. He had to be supervised at all times. One time I thought he was playing in his bedroom, but actually he had dangled himself out the window and dropped five feet to go outside and play. Thank goodness he wasn't hurt.

One friendship recently dissolved because my friend felt that if my child was unable to play properly with her kids, my family wasn't allowed to visit. I'd known this person since I was 13 years old.

My family still felt there was nothing wrong with my son. Even my family doctor stated that he was "just being a boy." After asking him for help and trying to explain that my son had behavior problems, my doctor said that he might be this way because he didn't have enough exposure to other children his own age, and, therefore, didn't know how to behave properly. The doctor recommended some books, but after reading them I felt more confused than ever.

The hardest thing for me was seeking out help without my husband's support. My mother was the only person in my family who encouraged me to get assistance.

SELF-DEFEATING THINKING

I honestly thought nobody believed me, especially my husband who didn't support me. I must be the only one in this kind of a mess. Frustrated and confused, I cried a great deal. I even went to the doctor's and got him to prescribe tranquilizers. Most of the time, I was unhappy and just wanted to escape because the situation seemed hopeless. It hurt a great deal losing friendships, and having other friends tell me I had a rotten child.

NEW THINKING

I saw an article in the local paper about parents who were having disciplinary problems with their children. Knowing I wasn't the only one having problems with my child was a tremendous relief. It gave me a new outlook for the days ahead. The article described a training program for the parents, to teach them child management skills. This I knew was for me.

EMOTIONAL RESPONSE

For the first time in a long time, I felt better and hopeful. There was a light at the end of the tunnel.

SOLUTION AND OUTCOME

I enrolled in a parent effectiveness training program. The program taught me different ways of dealing with my son. Instead of spanking, yelling, and flying off the handle, I was instructed to handle things with a calm approach. Also, I began to realize that good behavior came from praising the child, instead of focusing on the negative aspects all the time.

I was further instructed to give a command and explain to the child the reason why I wanted him to follow that command.

Every day was a struggle and mentally draining, but I felt I was changing my ways slowly but surely. When he misbehaved I gave him a command and, if he failed to listen, he was sent to his room. This was known as his quiet time. He understood that if he played nicely, he would be able to leave his room. It was truly working.

STICKING WITH IT

Some days it is hard because he pushes me to my limit. But the class has taught us the proper way to handle daily problems and it is bettering my relationship, not only with my son, but with my husband as well.

SLIPPING BACK

If I slip into my old ways and start yelling at my son, I'm a lot more conscious of my actions. The next time he gets into mischief, I try to correct myself. With practice it will eventually become "perfect."

Realize that you are not alone. No matter what your problem is, there are others in the "same cooker." Also, go for help because it is worthwhile and very rewarding. The caring and support I received was more than I could ever imagine. The program has changed my life for the better!

59: FAMILY VIOLENCE

Female, Age 28, Fitness Instructor

ADVERSITY

Violence in my household was a commonplace event when I was growing up. Every time my father got drunk, which was quite often, he'd be after my mother. I started to become more aware of it when I was in early grade school. My mother would leave him and I'd be forced to go to a different school for a period of time. Yet she always went back to him. I remember changing classes three times that year. Everyone was amazed I passed the grade.

The thing that finally got to me was when, as a teenager, I saw him come at my mother with a screwdriver trying to stab her. Most of the time, he was so drunk he'd just hit her with his fists, but this time I was really afraid he'd kill her. So I went flying out the door to the neighbors and called the police. I remember he tried grabbing at me to stop me, but I got past him. This was the first time the violence was directed at me.

For years I refused to date any guy the same nationality as my father. I was convinced it was just a way of life for "them." I became very independent not wanting to be like my mother, who always relied on my father for money to live on. She never worked, and he was always the breadwinner in the family.

I moved out of the house when I was in my late teens and was unable to stay with my sisters or brother for fear that my father would cause problems for them. They knew what he was like and had all lived through it and escaped by getting married.

For the longest time, I couldn't forgive my mother for dropping the charges against my father when he came at her with the screwdriver. In essence she made me to be the "bad guy" because I ran and informed the police. I hated her for not having enough guts to stand up for herself. I felt pretty much the same about my sisters and brother. They were opting out just to protect themselves. Instead, we should have banded together to stand up to him. Somehow I was made to feel that I had brought all this shame to the family for making it publicly known that our father was a drunk and a wife beater. As for friends, the few I had at school never knew about my problems at home. I didn't go out much so I never told them I wasn't living at home. To let on that my life was somehow different than theirs would be an embarrassment not worth risking.

SELF-DEFEATING THINKING

I kept justifying my anger toward the rest of the family by saying that they were all adults and should have taken better care to ensure that I wouldn't be subjected to violence in the home. I kept hearing them say that my father was a great person when he wasn't drinking. Somehow that justified their actions or lack of action. I kept telling myself that one day they would see they were wrong and how stupid their behavior was. I'd show them that I was right in leaving the house when I did.

NEW THINKING

I started spending a fair bit of time with my high-school guidance counsellor. He finally got me to realize that my family, mainly my two sisters and brother, were acting the way they were because of their own deep fears, which they had never resolved. They removed themselves from the house by getting married, but never really dealt with the fact that our father was a violent man. I started looking at it from their point of view and it was easier to forgive them. I never could justify my father's behavior, but I taught myself to be indifferent to it, otherwise it would cloud my judgment toward relationships in the future.

EMOTIONAL RESPONSE

I felt better not being angry all the time. I found that making new friends— namely, males—was easier since I had stopped sizing them up as potential wife abusers.

SOLUTION AND OUTCOME

I've become much closer to my sisters and brother now. I even started dating a guy of the same nationality as my father. Still I haven't forgiven my father's actions, but at least I can stand to be in the same room with him, and I've even spoken to him without being rude. My mother I now understand a lot better, and I don't hate her for putting up with my father.

STICKING WITH IT

Being able to think through why people act the way they do in situations helps me whenever I find myself getting all worked up about the injustices of life.

SLIPPING BACK

I tell myself that everyone in this world is different and they have a right to live their lives anyway they choose. People have a choice whether or not to stop the violence directed toward them. This mode of thinking relieves an anger that would otherwise eat away at me.

ADVICE FOR OTHERS

Think carefully before you act. Realize that people have the right to live their lives according to the choices they make. Finally, talk to someone, whether it's a counsellor as in my case, or someone else whom you trust and who listens well.

60: PURCHASING A HOME

Male, Age 39, Civil Servant

ADVERSITY

When I went to move into the house we had purchased, the previous owner had not moved out yet or even started to pack.

Due to the owner's recent separation, he was not thinking clearly and had not arranged to move anywhere. It was really hard on me and my family, because the owner spoke with all of his neighbors and asked if he could stay with them as we, the purchasers, would not give him an extension on the moving date. We felt like ogres in our new neighborhood. Also, I was constantly wondering what our family was going to do as we didn't have another place to live.

Buying a house, which was supposed to be a happy event, became very stressful. There was constant conflict between my wife and I. It also seemed that I was constantly complaining about it to our friends.

My work was affected in that I wasn't as productive. I was moody, my attention span became short, and things that were previously second nature to me, were now an effort.

SELF-DEFEATING THINKING

I was plagued by a constant panic, because I kept asking myself what was going to happen to my family and what legal steps I should take to get that guy out of our home. I really didn't know what to do next. It seemed the more I thought about it, the more I panicked. My wife bothering me about the children and their schooling didn't help either.

NEW THINKING

This was enough. I had to take charge. Things could not remain the same. I had stayed in limbo long enough. When I contacted my lawyer, he suggested that I involve the police. I then realized that I could have moved on this problem a lot earlier. It seemed that it took me a long time to get my act together because my panic had controlled my head, rather than my head controlling my panic.

EMOTIONAL RESPONSE

I felt a bit foolish, because I hadn't acted earlier. After the call to my lawyer, the stress level in our house went down considerably. I actually asked myself out loud why I didn't think of doing this before, since I deal with legal issues every day at work. But I guess when you allow yourself to be controlled by panic, you just don't think.

SOLUTION AND OUTCOME

The problem was out of our hands and in the hands of our lawyers. If I had to do this move all over again, I would have arranged for more time between leaving our old house and moving into our new one to allow for unforeseen problems.

STICKING WITH IT

After contemplating the outcome and how this problem was solved, I remind myself that remaining calm and thinking of a reasonable course of action is the best approach to dealing with this difficulty and any other problem.

SLIPPING BACK

I remind myself of how stupid I felt about not addressing this problem earlier. I just tell myself to settle down and think it out, instead of going into a great panic. It seems to work and a little humor doesn't hurt either.

ADVICE FOR OTHERS

The best way to deal with panic is to think with calmness and reason. Also, have your lawyer's number very handy. Allow a fair amount of time between your departure date and the possession date to cover any delays and difficulties.

61: CHILD WITH A SCHOOL PERFORMANCE PROBLEM

Male, Age 42, Carpenter

ADVERSITY

My daughter had not done well in 9th grade math and had to go to summer school in order to get an acceptable grade. In 10th grade I got a tutor for her and expected her to do really well. Naturally I was shocked when I found out at the end of the school year that she had failed this course. Math was absolutely necessary for future opportunities in college; therefore, our daughter had to repeat 10th grade math. This troubled our family because we had always valued excellence in school and now for the first time one of our children had failed an important subject. She knew I was very concerned about her math grade, but I tried not to let my disappointment show. Our daughter's peer relationships were strained. She didn't feel great seeing all of her friends go on to the next grade without any failing grades.

SELF-DEFEATING THINKING

I was initially horrified to find out that our daughter had failed, especially since I had hired a tutor. Was all of this my fault? Was I an ineffective parent? After all I never did well in math so maybe she inherited my problem.

NEW THINKING

I had to face this problem rather than look for someone or something to blame. My $100-a-session tutor had obviously not worked out. However, my most important realization was that my expectation may have been too high. My daughter clearly was not a math genius, yet maybe I expected her to be one. We decided after considerable discussion that she would not go beyond 12th grade math. Because her remaining grades were so good, she would not have difficulty pursuing a college career.

EMOTIONAL RESPONSE

I felt better now, but I won't be totally relieved until 12th grade math is completed.

SOLUTION AND OUTCOME

I introduced myself to my daughter's math teacher and kept tabs on how she was doing throughout the year, so as not to be surprised at the end of the year. Also, I got her a younger senior-high-school student to tutor her. This worked out very well. My only regret was not getting involved in my daughter's school career earlier.

STICKING WITH IT

I've become actively involved in my daughter's math work, and, because I don't want her to fail again, I'll stay involved.

SLIPPING BACK

I don't think that I'll slip into my old ways. Avoidance has never been a coping strategy for me. It was shocking at first, but after the initial blow, I've recognized the problem and I feel that I've dealt with it positively.

ADVICE FOR OTHERS

Identify the problem and carefully deal with it. Try to keep your child's feelings of self-worth up since it's easy for an adolescent to get low self-esteem. Keep involved in a non-nagging fashion. Finally, don't go around looking for someone to blame. That energy can be used more constructively in resolving the issue at hand.

62: MAJOR HOME RENOVATIONS

Female, Age 45, Dancing Instructor

ADVERSITY

I negotiated with a contractor to renovate the kitchen, the bathroom, and to add a family room to the existing house. The work started as scheduled in October, but after total destruction of the house, the delays began.

First the materials got delayed, then the contractor or the workers would not show. One time we arranged to be away for a full weekend, so the bathroom could be installed. When we returned Sunday evening, the fixtures were on the front lawn and nothing was installed. We had to call an emergency plumbing service to work through the night so everything could be hooked up. Apparently the contractor had gone home earlier without doing much work. Then he asked for more money to proceed. The final straw was when he fell down some stairs, suffered a concussion, and was hospitalized for six weeks. This delayed, by mutual consent, the renovations until after Christmas. We never heard from him again.

My personal life was a mess. The words "hate" and "kill" would always come to mind. It seemed he promised the world, but nothing happened.

The stress and strain were terrible. My husband and I both worked, so our spare time was limited. Nonetheless we would spend time chasing materials for the contractor only to find that they would be out of stock. Both of us felt that we were on a merry-go-round. The atmosphere, to say the least, was very tense.

Family was very supportive, offering us accommodation whenever we needed to escape. Our neighbors were very patient. It cost us a fortune to clean up the debris and dirt spread into their yards as a result of this renovation.

At work it was virtually impossible to concentrate because I worried about what was going on at home. Although my co-workers were sympathetic, they also wanted to see some productivity.

SELF-DEFEATING THINKING

I wanted to run, to escape somewhere—anywhere! My privacy was invaded and I couldn't find any place to sit quietly. The dirt and dust drove me to distraction; even our toothbrushes were dusty! The lies from the contractor were bizarre and I began to distrust everybody.

NEW THINKING

I developed a medical condition and that changed my thinking immediately. My doctor suggested we must do something or I might not live to enjoy the renovation. It became embarrassingly obvious that I was ruining my life over this. I finally reasoned that the worst that could happen to us was a loss of money.

EMOTIONAL RESPONSE

A great deal of relief. Also, I was anticipating our next steps.

SOLUTION AND OUTCOME

We hired a lawyer, fired the contractor, hired a new one, and within two weeks, we saw some big improvements. We got out of the house every Saturday and did something we both enjoyed. It was almost exciting to come home, as each day showed progress and you could see an end. The stress began to subside.

STICKING WITH IT

When we had to do further renovations, we made sure everything was in writing and we checked out personal references by visiting those people in their homes.

SLIPPING BACK

This too will pass, my sanity and health are much more important, after all it is only money.

ADVICE FOR OTHERS

Have everything, and I mean everything, in writing. Check personal references carefully, and work only with people whom you can like and with whom you can get along, as they will be around much longer than you expect. However, remember that your health and happiness are more important than any renovation that you embark upon.

63: SPOUSAL ABUSE

Female, Age 43, Accounting Consultant

ADVERSITY

My husband had a drinking problem. When he drank, and it was always to excess, he became bad tempered and violent.

Originally it was sporadic and each time I thought to myself that it was a one-time episode. However, it became a daily affair. I was very anxious and would worry about the house burning down, about his violent outbursts when I got home, and about his general state of mind. Over time I became more comfortable away from home.

As his abuse continued, I lost more respect for him. The love was not there emotionally or physically.

Friends ceased coming; only close relatives would visit despite my husband. Most people probably got frustrated by my passive acceptance.

With my work, I became less reliable and was often more tired in the morning. Because my office was in my home, I was usually interrupted by my husband. When we attended social events where clients or colleagues were present, my husband would be an embarrassment. I lost credibility with clients and colleagues, who probably assumed that if I couldn't get my personal life on track, how organized or professional could my work be? Others, I felt, were losing respect for me.

SELF-DEFEATING THINKING

I thought that since I was married to him the least I could do was help him. I felt slightly responsible for his actions. He probably wouldn't be in this country, like a fish out of water, if it wasn't for his marriage to me. He often blamed me for his situations and I accepted it.

In an ''abused'' state, you just don't think too clearly. I was just happy when things were okay for a day or so.

NEW THINKING

I began to realize that I was not helping him at all, that I was encouraging him to continue behaving in the same way. He didn't have to work; I was the breadwinner and I didn't put my foot down about any of his behavior. By being permissive, I was allowing it to continue. If things didn't change, then I wasn't fit to be a mother to our young child.

My husband didn't behave the way he did just because he blamed me or because he blamed the world. He was a drunk and he was unhappy with himself. Even when our child was born, and he felt that this was a wonderful event, he still went out and got drunk. After piecing my thoughts together, I knew that I would have to separate from him.

EMOTIONAL RESPONSE

I felt good about the decision, but felt shattered by the separation. Having turned into a "victim," I didn't feel very sure about the move. I was torn. To make matters worse, other problems arose that continued unabated. Questions of money, threats of kidnapping and violence, left me very paranoid. I used to jump when anyone knocked on the door.

SOLUTION AND OUTCOME

Slowly he began to have less of an effect on me, except with regard to our child. We had agreed that he would have our boy once in a while. But he continued to bring him home late or not at all, or he would be drunk on occasion and bring our son home.

This I was not prepared to tolerate.

STICKING WITH IT

It has become steadily easier. I am able to think ahead and plan my work and my life.

SLIPPING BACK

I catch myself when I don't insist on appropriate behavior. For instance when he brings our child home very late or if he's drunk, I tell myself I must act on it immediately—and I do. My old pattern could be described as too tolerant. I didn't like myself then.

Don't blame yourself for your husband's abusiveness because you will only reinforce his actions. Talk to someone who has been in the same situation. Or see an outside professional. It is very difficult to handle this on your own. Remember, you must act to break this pattern of abuse, otherwise you will constantly feel like a helpless, trapped victim.

64: DEATH OF A PET

Male, Age 13, Student

ADVERSITY

I loved my cat very much, but she became sick. She was very thin, losing hair, scrawny, and breathing short breaths. Our veterinarian said that she was too sick to be helped so he put her to sleep. I was down and feeling sick for three weeks. When I saw pictures of her, I wanted her back. When family or friends came over, I was irritable and grumpy. At school I had a very short temper and would talk back to the teachers. They weren't used to this because I had always been a well-behaved pupil. Also, my school grades suffered and went down, which concerned my teachers and my parents.

SELF-DEFEATING THINKING

I kept thinking that I would never have her back. I wanted her, but I would never see her again.

NEW THINKING

My cat was very sick and in pain, and it was not fair to keep her alive. I loved her so how could I let her suffer? We could not have fun together if she was sick.

EMOTIONAL RESPONSE

I felt better, but I still missed her.

SOLUTION AND OUTCOME

I got another cat that looked a lot like my first cat.

STICKING WITH IT

I remembered how much I enjoyed my other cat and looked forward to enjoying my new one.

SLIPPING BACK

The way I was handling it before was stupid. I wasn't being fair to my cat, my parents, and my teachers.

ADVICE FOR OTHERS

It's not fair for animals to suffer. There are other animals that need a good home. Just love them as much as you loved your first pet.

65: FAILURE TO GET ALONG WITH IN-LAWS

Female, Age 39, Private Daycare Operator

ADVERSITY

My problem was in dealing with my in-laws. They were, in my opinion, selfish people. When it came to gift giving, their favorite people became obvious. They would give their favorites wonderful gifts and the rest of us would get cheap little things.

Another problem occurred when my mother-in-law invited us for Christmas dinner. Both my husband and I turned her down for the dinner, but we said we would visit, as we were already invited for dinner elsewhere. When we arrived she had a big meal prepared anyway and was upset because we couldn't eat the meal. When my daughter asked for something to eat, she said, "No! Your mother has other plans."

This situation with my in-laws affected my life at home, in that I couldn't express my true feelings to my husband, because he would become upset and defensive. I also had to tell my daughters not to speak their minds about their grandparents when their dad was near.

SELF-DEFEATING THINKING

I knew as soon as I had contact with my mother-in-law she would say something to make me angry. She never thought I was good enough for her son. She never had anything good to say about any of her daughters-in-law, especially me. She treated me as if she deserved all the respect in the world and I deserved none.

I knew that when I tried to explain this situation and what I thought to my husband, he wouldn't understand. He would get hurt and upset and usually we would fight.

NEW THINKING

I decided that I had enough of the abuse. I just didn't want anything to do with my in-laws, particularly my mother-in-law, again. It was Christmas and I was going to enjoy it this time. I decided I would be happier at home by myself. My husband could take the children to see his mother if he so desired. I didn't have to see her so why put myself through it. I didn't deserve to be treated as a second-class person.

EMOTIONAL RESPONSE

I felt great, very relieved, as if a heavy weight had been lifted from my shoulders. I knew I wouldn't have to put up a front or make any excuses any longer. I knew I wouldn't have to listen to her complaints and her whispering behind my back.

SOLUTION AND OUTCOME

There was no longer any contact between me and my husband's parents. My husband and I don't talk about his parents and our feuding has decreased significantly. Our relationship is less strained and I feel better. My husband doesn't agree, but he respects my decision.

STICKING WITH IT

There really isn't any effort on my part at all. My life hasn't changed any except for the fact that I don't see them. I used to be all stressed out thinking about certain situations just before being with my husband's parents. I think that being with them wasn't worth the distress that I felt.

I now feel at peace with myself and with life, and I am proud of making a decision I believe is right for me.

SLIPPING BACK

I haven't been in direct contact with my husband's parents in a long time. I also don't feel a need to contact them. When my husband and kids go to visit, I sometimes get a feeling of panic, but then I remember that I am not going and this calms me down. I talk to myself out loud and give myself justification for my actions.

Having spoken to a lot of friends about this has also helped.

ADVICE FOR OTHERS

If you have to do something like this, decide if it's worth doing. I can't say my decision is right for everyone, but it worked for me. My advice is to consider all of your alternatives and then choose one that is best for you. You may have to compromise, but you shouldn't compromise to the point where you still feel miserable.

66: SINGLE-PARENT FAMILY

Male, Age 43, Contractor

ADVERSITY

One day my wife announced that she was leaving because of irreconcilable differences. I know I wasn't a perfect husband, but I never would have severed our marital relationship. She left accusing me of being too domineering, and psychologically and emotionally abusive. I was left to look after the children, who were seven and nine, the house, and my contracting business. My family and my friends were tremendously helpful, but they couldn't assist me in overcoming my strong sense of loneliness and anxiety about having so much responsibility resting only on my shoulders. Although I was able to work reasonably well and keep my clients satisfied, when I arrived at home I got very low and stewed about my capability as a single parent. It got so bad that I decided to get professional counselling, which was a wise move for me.

SELF-DEFEATING THINKING

I was outraged at my wife for doing this to me and our children. She should have tried harder to work out our differences. I didn't believe in divorce and I wanted her to abide by the same principle. Every time I talked to her over the phone, we started to quarrel and then I would shout at her and call her every name under the sun until she hung up on me. I kept thinking about what I could do to get back at her and make her life as miserable as mine. The longer I kept this up, the angrier I got. After the anger, I would get depressed and worry about how to get out of this mess.

NEW THINKING

I needed to know myself better and I needed to find out why the marriage failed. Also, I was prepared to spend the time, the energy, and the money necessary to get the counselling to uncover these mysteries. No longer was my pride at stake. More important, I wanted to understand who I was and what I could do to become a better person and a better parent.

EMOTIONAL RESPONSE

I no longer felt alone. Someone was in my corner helping me to help myself. There was delight in some family members becoming close friends, as well as disappointment in some friends distancing themselves from me. I felt love and support from some and a cool reception from others.

SOLUTION AND OUTCOME

I began to learn how to solve my personal problems. My awareness of others' impact on me increased. I was giving more consideration and time to what I said and how I said it. Antagonism was replaced by cooperation. When I spoke to my former spouse, the intense anger was no longer there. Our conversation was reasonable and focused mainly on the welfare of the children. Because I was more pleasant, I liked myself. How dumb I had been during my years of marriage, maintaining an over-inflated ego and a silly sense of pride.

STICKING WITH IT

I have tried to apply what I have learned about myself in as many situations as I can. Spirituality has also became more important in my life. It has offered me a greater sense of meaning. If my marriage had not collapsed, I might never have become a better person and a better father.

SLIPPING BACK

I'm disappointed, but I have learned to admit out loud to someone close to me that I slipped. By telling someone, I admit my vulnerability and my capacity to make a mistake. I refuse to berate myself as I did in the past. Instead, I accept my faults and try and learn from them. I attempt to recall what triggered my angry behavior and then document it for future reference. I then review what I have learned and think about how I could have handled the situation differently. This prepares me for a more positive response the next time a similar event occurs.

ADVICE FOR OTHERS

Learn as much about yourself as you possibly can. Take these new learnings and apply them as often as you can. Recognize that you are not alone in your struggles. Professionals, family, and certain friends can play key roles. Include spirituality in your life, you will find it an enriching experience. Being a single parent is difficult, but if you take advantage of the help and support that are available to you, difficulty will disappear. You will instead discover "a new you" and so will your children.

67: FAMILY ALCOHOLISM

Female, Age 27, Chartered Accountancy Student

ADVERSITY

Picture a typical small rural town, where a couple of teens get married; both are very poor with no job skills, and they proceed to have too many kids. The husband and the wife drink heavily, and with regularity, the husband mentally and physically abuses the wife and the children. The violent beatings result in the wife being hospitalized on more than one occasion. The children were terrified because of what they saw.

I began dating the oldest male child. I felt that I could help him see this was not a normal way of living. My family was very disappointed that I would get involved with someone who was very mixed up emotionally.

He was very possessive and used isolation techniques to try to keep me away from having contact with my friends.

SELF-DEFEATING THINKING

I had difficulty extracting myself from the relationship. This guy was developing characteristics of his father and I knew that before long he could or would use violence against me. I thought that I had no right to end the relationship. If I tried a little harder, maybe I could make it work. Also, I felt somewhat responsible for his younger siblings. I had a chance to develop some strong feelings for them. I thought by deserting him, I was condemning them to a very rough life.

NEW THINKING

I began to realize there is a fine line between helping someone and interfering. Caring for someone was not going to change his way of living. His problems were far beyond my limited experience of trying to help. Besides I valued my own health and safety.

EMOTIONAL RESPONSE

I still felt a bit guilty, but our lifestyles and goals were so different. Eventually I felt good that I was able to escape without permanent scars.

SOLUTION AND OUTCOME

After a very trying and tense conversation, I told him that I no longer wished to maintain the relationship. At first he became tearful, then I thought he was going to become violent, but nothing happened.

I got very involved in school activities, stayed away from any other serious relationships, and was very grateful to have a normal supportive family.

STICKING WITH IT

I am unlikely to associate with this type of family again. If I were to become involved with someone who displayed violent behavior, I could and would walk away without difficulty. I could tell this person he needed help that I couldn't give to him.

SLIPPING BACK

I remain very sensitive to family alcoholism and abuse, but remind myself that I cannot help because I am neither qualified nor able. The best that I could do is to direct them to professional help.

ADVICE FOR OTHERS

Leave the relationship as quickly as possible!!

THE DOMESTIC SOLUTION

The domain of marriage and family has certainly gone through its own up-heaval. Today, approximately one of every two marriages ends up in divorce. Fortunately, the institution of marriage has not been sacrificed altogether, because most individuals who divorce do get remarried. However, affairs during marriage are very commonplace. Most surveys indicate that 30 to 50 percent of marital couples include at least one spouse who has been, or still is, involved in an affair.

Family networks are evolving in interesting ways. Parents are living a lot longer, and because of their longevity, they require more care. As a result, parental care has become a major source of concern for many adult children. In addition to parental care, child care has become an ever-increasing worry, especially for those parents who try to remain devoted to their work and the long hours involved. Squeezed between children and parents, many people today are being forced to cope with seemingly untenable situations.

Demanding parents often transfer their "demandingness" to their children. With startling regularity children are suffering from anxiety, panic, worry, and the strong need to perform just to keep their parents happy. As a consequence, more children are now taking tranquillizers. Maybe in their tranquillized state, they will achieve what their parents want them to achieve.

The alcohol and drug scene is certainly alive and well, especially when it comes to teenagers. In fact, the incidence of teenage suicide has increased. Often drugs or booze are involved. Often teenagers who have attempted or committed suicide have left notes stating that their reason for doing so was that they felt alienated, not only from the rest of the world, but especially from their family and home environment.

The institution of religion has gone through a major transformation. Evangelism no longer occupies such a central position because of the apparent corruption that a number of prominent evangelists engaged in. People are still searching for spirituality, but many are rejecting the strong traditionalism and conservatism of the churches and synagogues.

Many adults are in a constant struggle to find that illusory "right mix" between the amount of time that should be devoted to work activities and the amount of time that should be dedicated to domestic activities. No doubt the struggle will continue, as many people have not discovered their ideal mix.

In these changing times, there remains a core of individuals who diligently pursue that delicate balance of health, happiness, and productivity. These are the "miracle makers" just described.

As members of society who may be grappling with similar marital and family issues, we would be wise to glean the key strategies highlighted in the preceding interviews.

Once again, our miracle makers employed a range of thinking tactics that altered their domestic lives. These people argued with themselves, and forced themselves to shift their attitudes. They put an end to their troublesome thoughts and resurrected a logic that launched their problem-solving capabilities. Then events began to turn around for them!

According to our miracle makers, they first committed themselves to thinking that created and then heightened the domestic mess—I can't accept reality, I can't deal with this fear and sense of doom, I am responsible for all my family's problems, I have to be in control of everything and know everything, I really don't have any problems.

Then these miracle makers changed the voices in their heads. They reorganized their personal philosophies of living—I refuse to let anyone make me unhappy or destroy me, I refuse to blame myself for others' actions, I'm responsible for my own actions and my own problems, certain things are out of my control, faith can be a positive influence.

If you had a choice to make, which line of thinking would you choose? The former or the latter? The answer once again is obvious—the latter. The inherent message is to carefully think about what you think. Be mindful of your mind. Commit yourself to thinking that will enhance your ability to be the best problem-solver you can be.

We indeed have an option in terms of how we think and how we manage our lives. These miracle makers shared their options and the dramatic results. The challenge is to adopt the option that will accomplish the same for us.

Once again, I am not proposing simple solutions to very often complex problems. But the miracle makers share very powerful tales about the influence that thinking can have upon health, happiness, and productivity. Grab hold of this approach—apply it and become your own domestic miracle maker.

PART 3

On the Personal Front

68: MAJOR PHYSICAL ILLNESS

Male, Age 42, Computer Technician

ADVERSITY

We were trying for a second child, with no results. At work I was in charge of a new area, with little support from upper management. Both of these ongoing situations certainly brought a great deal of stress and strain into my life.

I began to experience increasingly severe stomach pains and frequent high temperatures. I was hospitalized and immediately put into isolation where I felt like a leper. The first thing that came to mind was that it must be very serious, which obviously meant cancer. After three months in hospital and a bowel resection, I knew what I had alright, Chron's disease, an inflammatory bowel disorder that has no known cure. I was shattered to say the least. Being away for three months meant that I was cut off from everything and everybody. My home life consisted of visits from my wife and family. Granted I had a visitor every day and my wife was very supportive, but I was emotionally and psychologically isolated. More than that, I would have this illness for the rest of my life. I took various drugs for the disease, but they had bad side effects. I had dramatic mood swings and found that I was very short-tempered. Sure I could blame it on the disease, but I knew that it was linked to those pills I was taking.

In the hospital I found out who my true friends were. Some were delighted to see me alive, whereas others didn't even bother to visit. Because of my lengthy stay in the hospital, my chances for a promotion at work were permanently ruined. No longer would I even be able to move back into the position that I previously occupied. Most discouraging to discover was that people, especially at work, did not have a clue about my disease. They didn't understand, nor did they care to appreciate what this illness was all about.

SELF-DEFEATING THINKING

Over and over again, I repeated, "Why me?" I was now different and would be ill for the rest of my life. How would I ever cope? Fate had no right to do this to me!

NEW THINKING

I don't mean to sound trite, but after a great deal of soul-searching and intense discussions with my health care team and my wife, I realized that I could possibly get better. This was an illness that couldn't be cured, but could be controlled. Why waste my life in a state of depression, when I could still carve out a meaningful life for myself, albeit with certain limitations. With this renewed attitude, I committed myself to try and get better.

EMOTIONAL RESPONSE

I felt reawakened and reenergized. Yet my chief concern was the stigma of having this disease, once conversations about it arose at work. Also, and this was predictable, I continued to experience pain.

SOLUTION AND OUTCOME

I took a job with less stress, which also meant less responsibility. I saw my doctor often and started to feel better physically. My diet was altered considerably and I followed this new regimen religiously. Interestingly enough, my outlook on work changed. No longer did I have a burning desire and ambition to achieve. As I gained in strength, I still noticed that my energy level was not what it used to be.

STICKING WITH IT

I try to avoid situations that are stressful although I am not always successful.

SLIPPING BACK

I say that I refuse to let it worry or bother me. I try not to dwell on my difficulties, and I do not bring my work problems home with me.

ADVICE FOR OTHERS

With this problem you need to make some monumental changes in your outlook and lifestyle just to stay healthy and productive. Some of the changes may not seem worth it at the time, but they are worthwhile if they contribute to your continued good health. My advice is . . . don't worry—be happy.

69: NERVOUS BREAKDOWN

Male, Age 38, Electronic Technologist

ADVERSITY

I had a nervous breakdown. At the time I didn't know what was happening or what I was doing. It came on very suddenly and without warning.

It started at the singles club. There were rumours, so I isolated myself from these secretive conversations.

Sleeping became increasingly difficult and the less sleep I got, the more paranoid I became. I thought someone was going to kill me and constantly feared for my life. My delusions became more bizarre. Certain people were following me and these people were from my past, although I never knew them and they were really strangers in the present. As I was being taken to hospital by ambulance, I saw a connection between myself and Howard Hughes. We were very alike. When I arrived at the hospital, I finally felt safe.

SELF-DEFEATING THINKING

I had mental pain and physical pain. It seemed I couldn't walk on my right leg. This was later diagnosed as psychosomatic. I simply couldn't do a lot of things because I couldn't *think*.

My depression and deep shock were overwhelming because I was diagnosed as a borderline schizophrenic. A friend had this disorder and I wondered if I had to live the rest of my life like this.

NEW THINKING

I didn't want to be with anybody, but I thought that the only chance I had of getting better was to put myself in the hands of others. Others, namely doctors, would not make my decisions. I was willing to do anything because I had nothing to lose.

Initially I gave it time, because I knew that I would not rebound quickly. However, after many shock treatments, I decided that this was not the way

159

I envisaged my recovery. Hospital life was a terrible experience and I wanted out.

Now I was more determined than ever to go on with life even if it meant struggling with the most menial of jobs.

EMOTIONAL RESPONSE

I just hoped that everything would work out and felt determined to keep going and to keep trying to get better and better.

SOLUTION AND OUTCOME

I waited impatiently to be discharged from the hospital. So I started rug hooking and would walk around the halls for exercise. But I knew in the back of my mind that I would get back on my feet.

Finally, I was released from the hospital and referred to a sheltered workshop. Still under the care of a doctor, I was instructed to take certain medication. At the workshop, I worked six hours a day, but I really wanted to return to my previous job. Although my doctor did not support my decision, I returned to my old job. There I started to work only part time, from nine in the morning till noon. Because I tired easily, I would return home (which was still with my parents) and go to sleep. Eventually I worked longer and longer hours until I was back to a full-time schedule, but I made certain to stick to non-stressful work. It also helps to have a very obliging boss.

STICKING WITH IT

Well, I've had good and bad days. A number of times I've mistaken a cold or a flu for my illness and then would immediately want to quit my job. But after taking a couple days off from work, I'd return feeling better and wiser.

When the same episode happened a second time, I knew that I just had the flu and that it was not my illness returning.

SLIPPING BACK

I try not to work too hard and make certain to get enough rest and sleep. I use a variety of relaxation techniques to help me. For a long time now, I have not had any severe episodes because I recognize my symptoms. I had a couple of close calls, once at a flea market and another time at a shopping center, but I caught myself. The feelings of panic would flare up and just as quickly fade away. My insight into my illness gives me a tremendous control over it.

You have to accept the fact that you need help and may need it for a long time. If you can't, you won't get better. Try not to make rash decisions or take hasty actions.

If you have to take medication, be aware of what you take. If the drug is helping, insist it is helping and don't be afraid to say, "I want to stay on that medication, it helps me."

70: WAITING IN A LONG LINE

Female, Age 69, Retired Teacher

ADVERSITY

I've always hated lines especially at theaters and banks. In a crowded office or when I have to wait to see the doctor, I'm almost a basket case.

Throughout my career, I've been on time for everything and I guess I'm compulsively driven to be prompt. However, in today's society, it seems that lines are the norm and that they are accepted. Being of an older generation, I haven't come to accept this practice. Every time I'm caught between people, I get agitated and irritable. My intolerance of waiting, especially waiting for others, has resulted in some family quarrels. When a relative or friend is not on time, even if they were stuck in a line, they hear about it from me. Never have I hesitated to speak up and this has caught many a person by surprise.

SELF-DEFEATING THINKING

Why should I have to wait so long? Can't this person work faster or more efficiently like I did in my younger days! The doctor should schedule the appointments further apart. Why are professionals so inconsiderate, keeping a waiting room full of people who are tired of sitting around waiting to be called?

NEW THINKING

No new thinking. I accept myself the way I am. I'm not going to change and besides I don't want to change. Why do I have to compromise my position for another person's inefficiency?

EMOTIONAL RESPONSE

I take pride in my promptness and efficiency. I don't make people wait for me and I don't expect to wait for them.

SOLUTION AND OUTCOME

Before I used to get angry with people who kept me waiting. Now I still get angry, but at least I warn them in advance. I've been more open with people about my unwillingness to wait. Also, when I'm stuck in a line, I usually leave, but people usually know that I'm upset before I depart. If we don't take a stand, the lines will continue to grow and flourish and people will continue to settle for mediocrity in their work performance.

STICKING WITH IT

I know that others don't appreciate my approach and would prefer that I remain a little more relaxed and accept the wait you have to go through in a line. To them I say, "Balderdash!"

SLIPPING BACK

Do you mean have I ever waited patiently in a line? The answer is yes, but I don't make a habit of it! The odd time when I'm with a friend and we're carrying on an interesting discussion and we happen to be in a line, then I'll let it go by. Otherwise, lines are unacceptable.

ADVICE FOR OTHERS

Stick to your guns. It's easy to stand back in a line and wait like the rest of the crowd. But someone has to stand up and declare that it is unacceptable!

71: THE CAR BREAKING DOWN

Female, Age 27, Physiotherapist

ADVERSITY

It was early in the morning and I was on my way to work. Because it was winter, it was still dark. My husband had just purchased a secondhand car, and it was the first time I had driven it. Also, at this time I was five months pregnant. On my journey to work, the car kept stalling. In making a right turn, my car conked out right in front of a bus stop. Everybody was looking at me and no one offered to help. Then I saw a gas station at the corner and was quickly relieved. I went over to the gas station and asked the two attendants if they could tow my car because I had engine trouble. They could take my car out of the stream of traffic and bring it to the shop to see if it needed work. They refused. At first I was shocked. How could they say no? Then I became almost hysterical. I was expected at the hospital for an important appointment and here I was unable to get assistance from anybody.

SELF-DEFEATING THINKING

What is this world coming to? Here I am in need of help and no one gives a damn! The people at the bus stop didn't. What if I was being raped, would I get the same reaction? I was infuriated. How dare these idiots stand around and not offer a helping hand? The more enraged I became, the more time I kept wasting and the more out of control I felt.

NEW THINKING

I repeatedly whispered to myself, "Calm down, calm down, calm down." I had no choice but to accept this bad situation. I'm stuck here now, what can I do to get out of this mess? Being angry, resentful, and out of control were not making matters easier for me. The minute I directed my attention to doing something, I regained my focus.

EMOTIONAL RESPONSE

I regained my composure, felt more in control, and took responsibility for getting out of this mess.

SOLUTION AND OUTCOME

Instead of blaming others for my misfortune, I took complete responsibility. Remembering that my husband took his car to work, I called him from a phone booth. He arrived within a half hour and helped me to get the car to the gas station. There both of us decided that we would purchase a membership with the motor league. When I arrived late for work, no one believed my explanation. That was quite a memorable day.

About a month later, I was going to visit a friend and my car stalled again. This time I encouraged myself to remain calm and take control of the situation. I called the motor league and they were there within about 15 minutes.

It was still an inconvenience, but I certainly handled this same situation better.

STICKING WITH IT

I am generally trying to be more accepting of bad situations. Problems like this happen from time to time and I just have to do the best I can. Some problems you can't control like your car breaking down, and losing control doesn't solve anything.

SLIPPING BACK

First, I talk myself down! Then I leave the situation and take a few minutes to carefully think about the issue at hand. This has helped me to remain calm and collected and to problem-solve more effectively.

ADVICE FOR OTHERS

It doesn't matter what crisis it is, from your car breaking down to losing your wallet, staying reasonably calm will benefit you more in dealing with the problem than becoming upset and hysterical. In the back of your mind, you should always remember that it isn't the end of the world.

72: LONELINESS

Female, Age 29, Dress Designer

ADVERSITY

I was young and naive when I got married and didn't have much experience with men. After the marriage, many problems arose, especially financial ones. He didn't like to work, so the onus was on me to bring in the money. He would start a job and either quit or get fired after about a week. Being heavily on drugs didn't help his position. Unknown to me, my girlfriend and he got together and started a relationship. All of my friends knew about it, yet I was in the dark for the longest time. Because I trusted him and never believed that he would do such a thing, it took four or five months before I figured it out. When I found out about the affair, I left the apartment and went to stay with my parents. He remained in the apartment. This is when the feeling of loneliness started.

I stopped eating; I didn't go out anywhere and didn't even feel like returning to work. The lack of energy and lethargy were overwhelming. To think that I used to be so full of vitality because I thought that I was happy. Now everything had come to a standstill. I was alone with my intense feelings and thoughts—all of which centered on him. I loved the same music as he did; we had so much in common. Now that he was no longer around, it seemed that my identity had been stripped.

At home my parents were very supportive and caring, although at first I thought they would shout at me and declare, "I told you so," since they never liked him from the beginning. But they didn't. They tried to get me involved with my friends. They listened to me when I decided to open up, and they were basically there when I needed them. They even helped me pack the rest of my things at the apartment after my husband had abandoned the place without telling the landlord.

With my friends, I soon realized what true friendship was all about. Some ignored me altogether, while others made every effort to get me out and to make me as comfortable as possible under the circumstances.

SELF-DEFEATING THINKING

I constantly blamed myself. I wasn't good looking enough. I wasn't good in bed. I was too dominant because I earned the money and he didn't. Then I would start to feel sorry for myself. I must be the only one in this mess. No one knew what pain and grief I was experiencing. It was really hard because all I could think of was, "What did I do wrong?" I even thought of killing myself on occasion, because no one really knew about my inner turmoil and no one sincerely cared.

NEW THINKING

After months of being upset and crying, I shouted at myself, "Will this loneliness ever end?" I was finally convinced that I had to do something with myself. I was a big wimp.

I must now seize the opportunity and get on with life!

EMOTIONAL RESPONSE

I was awe-struck by this renewed energy and spirit.

SOLUTION AND OUTCOME

I bought new clothes and put new energy into my social life. After a period of time, I experimented with dating. My renewed interest in people was the signal that I was indeed a new person. However, the most significant revelation was that I didn't need to live with a man to be happy.

STICKING WITH IT

I returned to designing school and picked up many new ideas. This gave me more confidence at work. Remarriage was no longer an impossibility in the future. But most important was the fact that I was doing something for myself now.

SLIPPING BACK

I remarried and now have three children. A while ago, I would wonder, "What if my marriage failed again?" "Could I go through that again?" But I have a loving husband and great children and live life to the fullest. I can't predict whether it might happen again, but that's not important. What is important is living a full life now.

You have to take a good look at yourself. Only you can change yourself. Force yourself to get reinvolved in life.

73: BEING CUT OFF IN TRAFFIC

Male, Age 28, Sales Supervisor

ADVERSITY

It really bothered me when I was cut off in traffic, so much so that it affected my mood all day. One time this idiot cut it so close that I almost ran into a truck. I chased after that driver and if I would have caught up with him, I hate to predict what might have happened. For the rest of the week, I was impossible to be with. For the first time, I realized that maybe I had a more serious problem here.

SELF-DEFEATING THINKING

I didn't really think that my entire life was in a mess, but I knew that this was bothering me more than was healthy. I had no control over the situation and this is what troubled me the most. I was letting these episodes really get to me. I would swear and curse at other drivers and sometimes threaten to punch their heads in. What frightened me the most was that I wanted to hurt people.

NEW THINKING

One day I simply realized that no one was getting anywhere much quicker than I was and that it wasn't really worth creating extreme anger and frustration just to get to my destination a couple of minutes before the next guy. Why risk everyone's life by driving like a maniac? I told myself that I had to settle down while I drove and when I felt myself becoming aggressive and aggravated I would remind myself of my new outlook. I also made a conscious effort not to drive in rush hour, but rather walk or take the bus or subway.

EMOTIONAL RESPONSE

I felt relieved. This didn't happen overnight, but I soon realized that I was more relaxed when I drove.

SOLUTION AND OUTCOME

Basically, I was no longer as stressed out. My moods were not so up and down. Going through rush hour traffic no longer affected me in the same way.

STICKING WITH IT

This was simple. I always reminded myself of my logo: that no one was getting anywhere much faster than I was. I would drive safely and get to my destination maybe a little later. People who cut me off were not going to bother me!

SLIPPING BACK

I still let myself curse and swear at times, but I always think about my driving logo mentioned above.

ADVICE FOR OTHERS

Avoid driving at rush hour if possible. Have someone else drive occasionally. Remember that no one is going to arrive at their destination much quicker than you by cutting you off!

Drive safely, not vindictively—it just isn't worth it.

74: INTRACTABLE PAIN

Female, Age 29, Nursing Student

ADVERSITY

I was hit by a car on my right side a week before my nursing training in England. I was admitted to hospital for observation because of concern for a severe concussion. Nothing significant showed up and I was discharged, although I still was experiencing discomfort.

As my nursing training continued, the pain in my right loin region became more frequent. A few months later, I experienced low back pain as well. The low back pain progressed and made it difficult to get comfortable when sleeping. When I spotted blood in my urine, I reported to the hospital and was admitted for tests regarding a possible renal problem. The diagnosis was confirmed as tuberculosis of the right kidney. The course of anti-TB medications started, but failed because of my severe reaction to them. Further tests showed that the right kidney was atrophied and the right ureter was also involved. A right nephrectomy (kidney removal) and ureterectomy (ureter removal) were performed.

I tried to stay away from friends and family, not wanting to expose them to the TB germs, even though my condition was not contagious.

At first my family did not realize my condition because I tried to be as normal as possible. Eventually they found out and were very worried but supportive, especially after the operation. They looked after me very well indeed.

My friends who knew what happened were understanding and did not stay away from me. They tried to help in every way. I appreciated their concern and was grateful.

My nursing training was temporarily suspended during my convalescence. When I fully recovered, I returned to my training.

SELF-DEFEATING THINKING

Why did it happen to me? I was too young to lose my kidney and ureter. What if something happened to the other kidney? Could I lead a normal life again? One thing was certain, I would not marry and have a family. I would not burden another person or leave children without a mother. If I should die, would my parents be alright emotionally? If I had been diagnosed earlier, could my kidney have been saved? My mind was racing with these questions.

NEW THINKING

Of course there were no exact answers to these many questions. This was hard to accept, and yet I needed to accept it. I could still have a normal life if I was careful with my health from now on. My sister would look after my parents if anything should happen to me. I now needed to look ahead and not devote myself to worry but to living a full life.

EMOTIONAL RESPONSE

I felt at peace now that I have planned for the future.

SOLUTION AND OUTCOME

Once I had accepted my future, I returned to a "normal life" except that I was more conscious of my diet and I reminded myself to have lots of fluid. I would observe my ankles for edema (swelling) and reduce my salt intake. I took care not to overload my remaining kidney. I treasured each day as if it were my last. I had company more often and enjoyed their visits.

STICKING WITH IT

Life being so precious, I enjoyed what it had to offer. I became more sympathetic to other people's problems since we all fall victim to misfortunes. I understood what patients had to go through and tried to help them more.

SLIPPING BACK

When I felt depressed again, I would count my blessings and focus on how lucky I was to be rid of that disease.

ADVICE FOR OTHERS

If you experience pain, do something about it quickly. Seek medical consultation and hope that if you have an illness that it can be treated when it is still in its early stages. If you have to have surgery, do not be scared because it does not mean the end. Finally, live your life to the fullest every day, you never know what might happen!

75: DRUG ADDICTION

Male, Age 23, Laborer

ADVERSITY

When I was 12 years old, I wanted to be accepted by my friends so I started doing drugs. By the time I was 23, I was working in a factory and taking cocaine. It helped my backache, which I got from standing eight hours on the line. It also kept me awake when working nights. Because I would have trouble falling asleep, I would take other drugs to counteract the coke.

When I was high, I was on top of the world. I worked quickly and efficiently. At the same time, I lost a lot of weight. But I didn't care. I partied as often as I could.

My parents with whom I lived, didn't have a clue what I was up to. When I was really high, I managed to avoid them. After a while, work was getting to me because the supervisor was so demanding, pushing us to get the product out. Eventually I didn't care about my work. One night my girlfriend died in front of me. She overdosed on cocaine in her bathroom. That same night, I hit rock bottom in a jail cell.

SELF-DEFEATING THINKING

I had pain all over; I needed a fix. That's all I could think of. Also, I thought of killing myself. There was no other way to solve my problems. It was hopeless.

NEW THINKING

I spent a lot of time in a psychiatric ward. The staff helped me to start thinking more logically and positively. I made many friends there and started thinking better about myself. My family supported me when I transferred to an addiction treatment center. There they taught me to make positive changes in my life, to face my problems without drugs. I learned exercises to relieve my backache and promote relaxation. Instead of escaping responsibility and partying all the time, I concentrated on reorganizing my entire life. Months were spent in intensive treatment.

EMOTIONAL RESPONSE

I felt good about myself but afraid of starting my life over again. I managed to get a job in another factory, away from my "drug-crazy" friends.

SOLUTION AND OUTCOME

I worked days and slept well at night without the use of drugs. I continued my relaxation exercises and didn't go on partying binges which always wrecked me the next day. Interestingly enough, I managed to gain back all of the weight which I had lost.

STICKING WITH IT

I tell myself that I have learned to live without drugs. The first step is the hardest. The rest comes easier.

SLIPPING BACK

Whenever I think of taking drugs I think about dying. Like they say at the treatment center, take "one day at a time". When I have problems I try to talk to my family about them. I tell myself you can cope and help yourself or you can die. It's that simple.

ADVICE FOR OTHERS

Don't take drugs. Get help as quickly as you can from professionals. Do whatever they suggest because it really works. Also get rid of your friends who use drugs. They can only hurt you.

76: BEING TAKEN ADVANTAGE OF

Female, Age 44, Librarian

ADVERSITY

I was always known for having a "soft personality." My childhood and adolescence were largely influenced by my mother who would always give in to the demands of others.

When people called me to do something, whether I wanted to or not, I would always say "yes." Afterwards, I would get angry with myself for being so agreeable. Two friends would especially hound me and take advantage of my time and energy. As a result, my life was disorganized because the house was always a mess, my children felt neglected and my husband was frustrated. It just never occurred to me that I had a choice. I would often hear my husband say "no" yet this didn't seem to be in my repertoire. When these two friends requested my time, and they often insisted, I repeatedly gave in. Eventually, when I did become more assertive these so-called friends never saw me again.

SELF-DEFEATING THINKING

I was afraid to hurt people and was intent on pleasing them. If I remained helpful, I could never be criticized for being selfish and self-centered.

NEW THINKING

To come to grips with the hurdle of people taking advantage of me, I reached a crisis point of total physical exhaustion. With the help of my minister, I realized that I needed to be honest with myself. If people were going to upset themselves because my priorities differed from theirs, so be it. I had no intention of hurting others, but I did need to set aside time for my family and myself.

EMOTIONAL RESPONSE

I felt so much freer. A big weight had been removed from me.

SOLUTION AND OUTCOME

When someone requested an outing, I simply told the person I could or could not make it. By recognizing that I had choices, and could set priorities, I began to settle down and enjoy my life. But the first few times were not easy, believe me.

STICKING WITH IT

A great deal of self-discipline and spiritual support from my church have helped me not to be taken advantage of. But I remain vigilant and watchful for slip-ups.

SLIPPING BACK

When I notice myself slipping, I catch it more quickly. Then I can change my mind and get the message out to the other person. My husband also offers me gentle reminders.

ADVICE FOR OTHERS

Try to be honest with yourself and others. Make it clear, without being offensive, that your time is limited for outside activities. Good friends will understand your position; others who have taken advantage of you may not understand and may chose to terminate the so-called friendship.

77: NOT ACHIEVING YOUR PERSONAL GOALS

Female, Age 24, Dental Assistant

ADVERSITY

I went to college for dental assisting, planning to return within a year or two to become a dental hygienist.

After I started working as a dental assistant, I applied to the dental hygiene program but was rejected. Then I tried another college and got the same response. Rejection letters were all I saw for the next two years. It was clear that my grades were simply not sufficient to gain entry into the program.

But I was still obsessed with becoming an hygienist. What made matters worse was that a number of my friends were admitted to the program and yet I wasn't. They would eventually make more money and have great careers. Where was I?

I was a bitch most of the time. I'd get down on myself and also get very jealous of the hygienists in my office.

SELF-DEFEATING THINKING

My self-esteem was very low. I hated myself for not trying harder in school to get better grades. Everything I was doing seemed useless. I even started to hate my job.

NEW THINKING

It took some time but I got around to it. I started to examine people. I reminded myself that I was young, healthy, independent and had a decent paying job. There was no doubt that I was better off than some. My friends were great and rallied around me. They helped me to appreciate my many strengths.

EMOTIONAL RESPONSE

The pressure to get into hygiene was gone. The burden of defeat was lifted.

SOLUTION AND OUTCOME

I was happier. In fact, I started a new job. The staff was extremely friendly. My job began to hold meaning for me again. Also, I started to focus on myself . . . new hobbies, exercise.

STICKING WITH IT

My new job helps because I'm happier there. I can always apply to hygiene school next year or two to three years down the road. But more important, the fact that I may not become a hygienist doesn't really bother me anymore.

SLIPPING BACK

I start to focus on other goals I want to reach in life. I keep myself busy. Most important, I'm not in such a hurry to achieve all of my goals at once.

All you can do is try your best, but be satisfied with other significant things in your life, particularly your health and your family. Focus on other interests and aspects of living.

78: ALCOHOLISM

Female, Age 40, Student Law Clerk

ADVERSITY _____

A number of years ago I nearly died from alcoholism.

I'd always been insecure and doubted myself. My husband was a lot older than me, and he was in management. I was the manager's wife, entertaining a lot—cocktail parties—that's how I started to drink.

Drinking gave me confidence, so I drank more and more. I loved the socializing, the parties, the fun. Then I crossed the line and was drinking every day, hiding booze, to the point where I couldn't control it.

Then one New Years Eve, I said, "That's it, I need help!" I went to Alcoholics Anonymous (AA) and quit for 13 months. During that time I was never at home, always at AA meetings. So, one day my husband dumped me. He took up with my cousin. I was told to leave with my son so his girlfriend could move in. Too afraid to stand up for my own rights, I left. I had a job, but I couldn't hack it by myself, so I started drinking again. My license was eventually taken away for drunk driving. My mess wasn't fair to my son so I turned him over to my husband. Then the bottom fell out.

I went from job to job, started hanging around with people who loved to drink and lived with different guys, all of whom were alcoholics. Needless to say, these relationships never worked.

Into treatment I went for approximately four weeks, but about one month later, I returned to the bottle. My blood pressure went sky high and my family doctor finally admitted me to a hospital that treated my physical problem as well as my drinking. There I fell in love with my attending psychiatrist, who unfortunately left the hospital to pursue his practice elsewhere. I became extremely frightened, alone, and very depressed to the point where I tried to kill myself.

Recovered from my attempted suicide, I discharged myself from the hospital and headed straight for the bars. Drinking, not getting help, was all that mattered at this point.

Then I met Bill. He was an alcoholic, but not an obvious one. We lived together and drank steadily together. At this point, I was on welfare, but Bill had a constant supply of money. For all I know, he was independently wealthy. We bought cheap clothing and cheap food, but had a constant supply of whiskey.

I lived with him for a year and a half. On New Year's Eve, he died of a blood clot in his lung. I was too sick and always too hung over to mourn his death. Drinking was now constant, right up to bedtime. There were also three ounces of whiskey at my bedside, so when I got up in the morning, I would have my shot to straighten me out.

Eventually I couldn't even walk, let alone keep track of the days.

SELF-DEFEATING THINKING

I was desperate and worthless. My state of mind was so confused and bewildered that I assumed everyone would be better off if I was dead. I thought that I was drowning and could not pull myself out. Booze had a hold of me and without it, I couldn't see myself living. When I was uptight, it calmed me down; when I was shaky and dizzy, it straightened me out. Without booze, I was like garbage; with it, I was human again. As long as I had my alcohol, I could be with other people, otherwise I was terrified of them. But everything was lost—my job, my home, my marriage, my car, my son. I didn't have clothes to wear, but I would wander around my room half naked filled with whiskey. Every penny I had went for booze.

NEW THINKING

The day Bill died at my feet, I was so weak. I myself was dying, but I thought that I had the flu. My bowels were no longer under my control. When our boarder finally arrived, he saw Bill was dead and told me. The police arrived and found me fading in and out of consciousness and jaundiced. They forcibly admitted me to the intensive care unit of the local hospital. After about two weeks, I became aware of my surroundings. I had Alcoholic Neuritis, couldn't use my legs, and weighed slightly less than 99 pounds. Many a specialist examined me and one stated that I would never walk again. That's when my determination returned. I repeated to myself that I would walk again, just watch me. Although they claimed that I had destroyed too much of my brain, I was convinced that I would not spend the rest of my life in a wheelchair. First, I took physiotherapy and then was sent to my brother's house where, with constant effort and work, I eventually walked again.

Because Bill had died and I had come so close myself, I knew I had to stop drinking. Bill's death signalled a message to me. Die or get my shit together. Now that I had lost everything, there was nowhere to go but up.

EMOTIONAL RESPONSE

I was desperate to get on with real living once again. Now that I could finally walk, I felt more positive about my future. I was determined to reinstate my license so that I could feel like a member of society. I was no longer absorbed by self-hatred, but instead by a desire for self-fulfilment.

SOLUTION AND OUTCOME

I got my licence and then returned to school, although I was scared to death. To this day, I still doubt myself somewhat. Sometimes I get so scared, I cry and wonder what I'm doing. But I tough it out and I guess that's the main difference.

STICKING WITH IT

When I get anxious and really uptight, I hang on and know that it will eventually pass. I watch T.V., go for a walk, and even meditate. To relieve some of my pressure, I dropped one of my college courses and that helped considerably. However, the real difference is that I'm aware I'm walking a tightrope and that I'm the only one who can relieve my pressure.

SLIPPING BACK

Twice last summer I drank. Once was when I thought I had breast cancer. The other time was in celebration, when I found out that the lumps were benign. The second time I drank all night. This scared me half to death, because I thought that I would only have a couple of drinks, but hit five bars instead and got plastered. I literally couldn't stop. Then I realized how strong my addiction really was and how easily I could slip into my old ways. But when I remember where I was, I don't ever want to return to my old lifestyle. The fear of slipping back keeps me abstinent.

ADVICE FOR OTHERS

You must accept and admit to yourself that you are an alcoholic. Until you accomplish this, you will not change your life. The rate at which you lose important parts of your life will more than likely determine how quickly you admit that you are an alcoholic.

Try Alcoholics Anonymous. Although I didn't stick to it, I recommend it highly. Talk about your addiction even if you are ashamed of it as I was. When you decide to pull yourself together, set reasonable goals and as you reach them, you will feel better. Then set new ones. However, don't set goals that are out of sight. You don't need to add any more frustration into your life.

79: DAUGHTER MOVING AWAY

Female, Age 59, Supervisor, Accounts Payable

ADVERSITY

My daughter moved to England. She was not only my daughter, but my best friend as well. During my traumatic marriage breakup, she was most helpful and acted very much like a mother figure to me. Had she not been around at the time, I might have crumbled under the pressure.

Her husband had received a very good business offer that required considerable travel and relocation to London, England. After much soul-searching she decided that they should go.

At first, I was devastated, thinking that I would never see her again. I went into a state of crisis similar to the one I was in when my husband first left me.

My family was very concerned. I tried to keep busy by socializing a great deal, but I was constantly anxious and hyperactive. When I went out with my girlfriends, I would start to get chest pains thinking about being alone after the evening was over.

My work became a lifesaver as I was able to go there and keep busy for eight hours and not think about my home life. My peers didn't really know what was going on, as I put on "a good face" and kept my thoughts and feelings to myself.

SELF-DEFEATING THINKING

I kept worrying about what I was going to do without her. At the same time, I couldn't seem to think for myself and became awfully dependant, as well as very forgetful and absent-minded. I was convinced that I had lost my daughter and that her husband, who was now "the enemy," would never let her see me again.

NEW THINKING

One unhappy Sunday, it struck me that I could visit her if I wanted to. It was not as if she had left the earth. Shortly thereafter, my daughter called me one evening and invited me to London. She and her husband sent over a return ticket. I went over and stayed for two weeks and had a delightful time. Knowing that I could visit her by simply hopping on a plane made a world of difference. Also, recognizing that a loving relationship does not have to diminish because of distance was most important.

EMOTIONAL RESPONSE

My outlook on life became much better. I was most hopeful that I could see my daughter whenever the strong need arose.

SOLUTION AND OUTCOME

I now began to plan for my next trip to London. My daughter was pregnant and carrying my first grandchild. We traded many phone calls and she often would ask for my advice. These conversations were most heartwarming.

STICKING WITH IT

Well, I realize now that people can't stay and be with you forever. They can't always be what and where you want them to be. My other daughter recently married and moved away a short distance from me. If I would have applied my previous thinking, I would be fretting and worrying forever.

SLIPPING BACK

Everyone slips don't they? I just keep myself busy with friends. We go out and enjoy one another. They are a great source of comfort and support. I am more content with myself now.

ADVICE FOR OTHERS

Learn to have confidence in yourself. It's the most important of all. Keep in touch with those who have moved away because they really love to get news about what is going on. They are lonely and miss you as well. Don't always give them bad news about how miserable you are at home. Liven up the conversation with a little humor and silly stories. Provide them with a happy and meaningful exchange, and they will keep writing and phoning.

80: WEIGHT PROBLEM

Female, Age 36, Systems Analyst

ADVERSITY

Two events or situations coincided that contributed to my rapid weight gain. I had abdominal surgery for removal of my gallbladder, which resulted in decreased activity. In addition, I ate more because foods that could not be tolerated before the operation could now be eaten. At the same time, I was experiencing problems in my marriage, and found myself eating when I felt sad, lonely, or hurt.

The marriage ended and my husband blamed my overweight condition for his departure. Following this, on my own with a small child, I stopped cooking meals and ate prepared foods instead. My activity level became even lower.

After the separation, I found it difficult to relate to people, thinking that they wouldn't want to have anything to do with me.

My increased weight made me more sedentary, and I didn't do things with my child that she would have liked me to do. I would promise to have fun with her and not follow through, and then feel guilty and eat more.

My father teased me about my weight gain, which created even more emotional turmoil for me. As my weight continued to increase, I found that I didn't feel well, and that I had low energy, poor concentration, and poor memory.

Due to my low energy and my concentration and memory problems, my work suffered considerably, causing frustration for my co-workers. Eventually they became angry and demanding, putting more pressure on me.

SELF-DEFEATING THINKING

I talked to myself about what I was doing wrong yet still kept doing it. "I know I shouldn't be eating this or sampling that," were conversations I would often have with myself. But I told myself that I would change tomorrow and take the easy way out by stuffing my face. I was the expert procrastinator.

NEW THINKING

Initially, my thinking started to change after having a checkup with my family doctor and finding that I had an elevated blood-triglyceride level. At that time, my doctor told me that if I didn't lose weight and change my habits, within five years I could have a heart attack or stroke. This made me realize that I had a problem, but I still felt inside that "it wouldn't happen to me." Nonetheless, I went for monthly visits to the hospital dietitian, but it was just going through the motions, mainly to please my doctor. I persisted in going month after month, even though my weight didn't go down, and sometimes it even went up. Eventually I began to feel humiliated by the exercise and gradually came to realize that this was my problem and I was the only one who could change things. When I finally accepted this responsibility, I became committed! I joined the Weight Watchers program, and would not eat any non-diet foods.

EMOTIONAL RESPONSE

In a word, fantastic. I felt good about myself, even felt beautiful, and very proud of my commitment. My improved self-image and increased self-esteem gave me renewed confidence that I would be able to accomplish my goals.

SOLUTION AND OUTCOME

I started organizing my life. My regimen required planning and this included time for meal planning, shopping, food preparation, and cooking. I found that I now had the energy to accomplish this.

STICKING WITH IT

There have been some serious challenges. At times when there are problems at home, such as emotional issues left unresolved, I find that I slip back. However, my new wardrobe gives me instant feedback so that I can't deny if the problem is recurring.

SLIPPING BACK

I look for motivation from other "losers," friends who have lost weight. My daughter is a constant support.

ADVICE FOR OTHERS

You have to do it for yourself, not for anyone else. Don't let anybody put you down for doing it. Some people, for whatever reason, will try to deter you from changing and you will have to be convinced that you are serious in your attempt, because procrastination comes from lack of conviction.

81: FACING SERIOUS SURGERY

Female, Age 43, Hydro Commissioner

ADVERSITY

I had a hysterectomy earlier, yet had continuous bleeding for the longest time. Despite undergoing several procedures that were meant to bring it under control, including a D and C, I found I continued to hemorrhage. Not only was I fed up with the situation, but I was also continually tired from the blood loss.

After I had worked out the pros and cons of the recommended surgery, which was considered to be most serious, I reached the conclusion that it was just about the only option I had under the circumstances. My next concern was with the anaesthetic. You see, I'm a heavy smoker, and smoking and anaesthesia don't really mix very well.

How did the pending surgery affect my life at home, my personal life? Well, to tell you the truth I was going through peripheral marriage problems at the time and it was difficult to differentiate what was bringing on and causing my anxiety.

SELF-DEFEATING THINKING

I was concerned about the aftereffects of the anaesthetic. Of course, I also worried about the "finality of it all," should something serious happen during the operation. Once the uterus was out, the ability to have children would be removed forever. I was still young enough to have children, but up until now the decision not to have any was more out of choice. As with many women, the ability to bear children was important to me. Also, I dwelled on the possibility that the surgery would negatively affect my sex life and my femininity. This tied in significantly with the marital problems I was coping with at the same time. My mind was certainly overwhelmed with worry.

NEW THINKING

This was a "no-choice" situation. I had to come to terms with having the surgery, because if I continued to procrastinate, the quality of my life was going to deteriorate. It was really a case of getting on with it as soon as possible. There really didn't seem to be any alternative.

EMOTIONAL RESPONSE

At the end of the day, I came to the conclusion that there was no alternative and once I came to terms with that, I felt almost a sense of relief. I almost felt like saying, "let's get on with it."

SOLUTION AND OUTCOME

Once I realized that TINA (Margaret Thatcher's favorite expression, "There Is No Alternative") situation, I found I could carry on with my life much better. I wanted to have the surgery as soon as possible, hopefully recover quickly, and live my life as before with the same amount of energy.

STICKING WITH IT

Although my fears were very real, the result of the surgery was very positive. None of my fears materialized. I recovered well from the anaesthetic despite being a heavy smoker, the surgery did not adversely affect my sex life or my femininity, I felt much healthier and stronger, and I haven't had any regrets about not being able to bear any more children.

SLIPPING BACK

I remember Maggie Thatcher's favorite expression—TINA.

ADVICE FOR OTHERS

Don't procrastinate. The sooner it's done, the better.

82: FEELING OUT OF CONTROL

Female, Age 38, Engineering Student

ADVERSITY

In retrospect, I can say that there were too many changes in my life. My old boyfriend had gone. My father and niece had both died suddenly. I had given up my profession and steady income and was in the middle of completing a four-year engineering degree that was extremely difficult. I was involved in a new relationship and was contemplating marriage.

My first panic attack occurred after we had my future in-laws for dinner. They had left, and my boyfriend and I had gone out for a walk when I felt a sudden loss of control over my emotions and actions and a paranoia about people in the street. I felt like I was falling apart. I needed to get home before I did anything foolish.

These attacks began to occur several times a week. They occurred in the subway, in the university cafeteria, while out shopping or in the company of friends. I began to get nervous about going out in case I had an attack and embarrassed myself, particularly in front of strangers. I was in constant fear of losing control to the point where I developed a fear of the fear itself. It was a never-ending cycle. I was continually wired up and caffeine accentuated my symptoms. Eventually I went to my family doctor and got a prescription for tranquilizers. However, my concentration was dwindling and my productivity at school was declining. I began to withdraw from situations, but never from the friends whom I thought could be supportive. I was told that for a number of months I didn't laugh and hardly even cracked a smile.

SELF-DEFEATING THINKING

I was terrified of losing control because I might never regain it. I was convinced that it would never go away and would remain to haunt me for the rest of my life. Imagine the thought of losing your mind. Well, that was with me almost every day. Also, I was very conscious of the many decisions facing me regarding career, marriage, lifestyle.

NEW THINKING

If a panic attack happens, it is not the end of the world—I will live through it. This thought was a lifesaver. Also, I began to accept my limitations. I recognized that possibly my many aspirations were unrealistic and were contributing to my anxiety. In taking stock of myself, certain aspects of my life would need to slow down, namely the pursuit of a new career and the pursuit of marriage.

EMOTIONAL RESPONSE

I felt somewhat less anxious and more in control. However, this didn't mean that my panic attacks stopped.

SOLUTION AND OUTCOME

Deep breathing, concentrating on something else, or removing myself from the situation were all strategies that helped. Wherever I went, I took a book with me and would force myself to read it whenever I felt an attack coming, such as on the subway. As I controlled my behavior and managed my attacks, my self-confidence improved steadily. Throughout this period, my books and tranquilizers were my security blanket. Although I did not often take Valium, I knew that it was available. One time, I consulted a psychoanalyst but became annoyed that she wanted to delve into my past and had no suggestions on how to presently handle my problem.

STICKING WITH IT

The more control I exert over the attacks, the less often they occur. I truly no longer fear an attack. If it should happen, it will not do me any lasting harm.

SLIPPING BACK

I immediately get myself out of the situation. I give myself pep talks. I tell myself that this will pass.

ADVICE FOR OTHERS

Get professional advice. Medication helps on occasion. Talk to others who can help you control the attacks. Do not try to hide the fact that you suffer from panic attacks, because then you become paranoid. Get used to talking to yourself in a realistic and rational manner.

83: RETURNING TO SCHOOL

Female, Age 38, Radiology Technician Student

ADVERSITY

I had been working as a registered nursing assistant and was getting very bored with this job. Doing this for 12 years was degrading, especially when newly graduated nurses were put in charge over me and I was more experienced and knowledgable than they were.

On a whim I applied to the local college for the radiology technician program to see if I would be accepted. I was and then I felt there was no turning back.

Returning to school affected my personal life a great deal. Now that I no longer worked on a full-time basis, my income was considerably reduced, although I did receive a government grant and loan. Because studies occupied most of my time, the pursuit of an active social life was constrained, to say the least.

At home, my life with my roommate became strained. She worked full time and because my income had been greatly reduced, picked up a lot of the expenses that we had previously shared. Initially my roommate didn't appear to mind, but when I was into my second year she obviously started to become very resentful of this situation, which created a great deal of tension between us.

My family was very supportive of my endeavor to return to school. While at school many new friendships were established, especially with other mature students, as we had so much in common. My casual work as a nursing assistant was becoming more difficult to manage as my schoolwork and studying increased. But I needed the extra bit of money, so my studying suffered.

SELF-DEFEATING THINKING

I often thought how difficult it was to readjust my lifestyle. Had I made the right decisions? I was so used to living a carefree life, yet here I was sacrificing my independence. Returning to school full time required a lot of self-discipline and this was difficult for me.

187

NEW THINKING

I kept reminding myself that I had returned to school to better my situation and become a member of a profession I really enjoyed. This commitment was made to myself. It became a matter of pride to see it through and to succeed. Most important was knowing that what you want and are committed to does not always come easily.

EMOTIONAL RESPONSE

Once I accepted my full commitment to this endeavor, I began to feel much more determined to succeed. This was something I had to do on my own.

SOLUTION AND OUTCOME

Having changed my frame of mind from uncertainty and self-doubt to optimism and determination, I found going to school was actually becoming pleasurable. Being a student again could indeed be fun now that the pressure I had created seemed reduced.

STICKING WITH IT

After I graduated, I took this optimism and determination to my first position as a radiology technician. If I was able to return to school and graduate, then I could handle the challenges involved with my new job and new responsibilities.

SLIPPING BACK

I keep telling myself that quitting or giving up when in a difficult situation is the easy solution, but that it is not the best solution or one that I would be happy with. If I managed to return to school and graduate, then I can succeed in other difficult situations I might find myself in.

ADVICE FOR OTHERS

Others who wish to return to school should not wait as long as I did. The entire experience would have been easier for me if I had enrolled in school sooner. Many years were wasted working as a registered nursing assistant. That's the price I had to pay for postponing my decisions to return sooner because I was afraid of hard work and worried about my routinized life being disrupted.

84: MAJOR PHYSICAL HANDICAP

Male, Age 28, Human Resources Trainee

ADVERSITY

I have cerebral palsy and I am confined to an electric wheelchair. I have limited upper body and upper limb movement, but am able to write legibly and type slowly. There is also limited lower limb movement. Help with cooking, dressing, getting in and out of bed, and using the washroom is required, so an attendant is available in the apartment around the clock. At work I have an attendant come in twice a day to help me go to the washroom, therefore, I must control my fluid intake to live within these limitations.

Cerebral palsy is linked to a lack of oxygen to the brain cells at the time of birth. At one or two years of age, my parents took me to a medical center because I wasn't walking and my muscle coordination was very poor. My parents, who were Italian, really didn't understand English very well at the time, and struggled to find out what was wrong with me. Finally, I was diagnosed and my parents were instructed to take me for physiotherapy each day. However, this arrangement was not satisfactory. So it was recommended that I move into a long-term care hospital where all the necessary services could be provided. For 16 years from the age of three, I remained in a hospital. There I lived with 85 other disabled residents. I was introduced to my first wheelchair, which at that time was a manual one. Every weekend and on holidays, I would return home. But as I grew more comfortable with the people and my surroundings, I returned home less and less. It became apparent that my key support group was not at home, but was at the hospital. My bond with the other residents strengthened and my relationship with my parents weakened. They were struggling with the English language at the same time that they were wrestling with my disability. The combination was overwhelming to them, so they came to the hospital rather infrequently. My two older sisters seemed to accept my disability, but only came to visit me when it was convenient for them. On occasion, my sisters didn't even invite me to family functions. The closeness between my immediate family and me was no doubt waning.

My schooling till eighth grade was provided at the hospital. From ninth grade to the end of 12th, the other residents and I went to a regular high school. Special attendants came to assist us with our coats, books, lockers, and washroom activities. Ninth grade was a tremendous adjustment for me, since I was attending an able-bodied school, yet I myself was confined to a wheelchair. Yet I managed and then graduated to a community college. I found an apartment with 24-hour attendant care. The Government Ministry of Community and Social Services was most helpful and arranged to have a number of devices set up in my apartment so that I could live more comfortably. Also, outstanding rehabilitation counsellors were available to me for guidance and support.

SELF-DEFEATING THINKING

Overcoming a disability, especially one you have lived with all of your life, did not entail a sudden shift from negative thoughts, but a gradual progression towards self actualization and independence. When I began to learn about my body and what it could and couldn't do, was when I began to worry about what would happen to me. What would I be like when I was old? What kind of life would I have?

When I knew that I would never walk, I don't think I was really depressed. If you haven't experienced something, then how do you know what you are missing? There was no point in being depressed, because I had always been this way. But there were many times when I screamed and shouted in frustration, because I couldn't go to the washroom when I wanted to. I would get upset when there was no one around to help me and when I thought about my poor family relationships. If I could get into my bed when I was tired or take off my own clothes without an attendant, that would be great. These were my weakest moments. Occasionally, I asked myself, "Why me? Why did I have to be this way?"

NEW THINKING

After the new experience of going to high school and realizing that there was a life beyond the hospital, I knew then that I could survive in the outside world. I believed that I could cope in this able-bodied society. Although I was constantly surrounded by strangers, I told myself that they were just like me in many respects. Also, I reminded myself to ask for help because I couldn't assume that others knew that I required assistance. I was never shy or passive because I would never get anywhere if I was. The more I accomplished, the more I believed I could accomplish.

EMOTIONAL RESPONSE

I was very inspired. My confidence and self-esteem blossomed. I was learning, meeting new people, and surviving in a world that was not confined to wheelchairs. It seemed that the more I felt able to look after myself, the more fun and enjoyment I could experience in life.

SOLUTION AND OUTCOME

Although I was in a wheelchair, I did not believe that I was confined. Because I so much wanted to take advantage of life and explore new horizons, I refused to sit back and wait for things to happen. I made things happen.

STICKING WITH IT

I set targets for myself and make certain that I can indeed achieve them. There is nothing more frustrating than a goal that is too unrealistic. My ambition was to get a personnel position and I was able to obtain it in a government department. Also, I regularly remind myself how well I have done—I am reasonably independent, living in my own apartment, paying the rent, and enjoying life.

SLIPPING BACK

When I start feeling sorry for myself, I talk to my girlfriend, who is also in a wheelchair, and she tells me to smarten up. She helps me to see things differently. Many times I can handle situations on my own, but it sure is great to have her in my corner.

ADVICE FOR OTHERS

It is very important to be surrounded by stable people who care, who want to teach you, and who accept you unconditionally. To have goals is crucial, because there is virtually no point to living if there is nothing to do or to achieve. This is what life is all about whether you have a disability or not. Certain people haven't done well in life because they didn't have that burning desire to make things better, to go after what life has to offer. That's how my story ends—I went after what was offered to me!

85: BEING ASSAULTED

Female, Age 29, Bar Hostess

ADVERSITY

After work one night, my girlfriend and I decided to stay in the bar for the evening. Two unsavory looking men joined us and although I tried to discourage them from staying with us, my girlfriend took the opposite approach and was most encouraging. The men, both of whom looked somewhat drunk, said there was a party at their house and invited us to go. Although I tried to talk her out of it, my girlfriend said yes and got up with the two men and left. Afraid to let her go alone, I went along to protect her. She left in her car with one of the men and I got into the other man's car and all of us drove off.

We came to this dark house, parked the cars and went inside. All I wanted to do was convince my girlfriend to leave, but it was too late. She was already in a bedroom with the first man. I called upstairs but was suddenly grabbed from behind. The man threw me over his shoulder and although I kicked, screamed, and punched, this gorilla moved up the stairs to his room, locked the door and threw me on the floor. Then I knew that it was futile to fight and only hoped that he wasn't going to hurt me. He ripped off my clothes and proceeded to rape me. I remember nothing after that until I left the house. It was like I had experienced a catatonic stupor. There was no one I could talk to. The only person I was close to was my aunt, who was a French Catholic nun and would be horrified, to say the least, if she heard. She would never understand!

SELF-DEFEATING THINKING

I had been a virgin when this happened and believed that no man would ever want to marry me. I was dirty and now was afraid of sex. How would I ever form a meaningful relationship with a man? I was so distressed that I went for counselling, which helped considerably.

NEW THINKING

With support and counselling, I began to accept the fact that it was nothing I had done to bring this on. It simply happened and there was no reason to believe that it would happen again.

EMOTIONAL RESPONSE

I no longer felt dirty and tarnished. I could hold my head up and recognize that it was a one-time event.

SOLUTION AND OUTCOME

The police were never involved, because I did not want to draw attention to this mess that was behind me now. Eventually I got married and opened up to my husband. Outside of the counsellor, he was the only other person who knew of the rape. However, my sexual relationship with him was poor. To begin with, he was inexperienced and also couldn't accept what had happened to me. Our inadequate sexual relationship led to the downfall of our marriage. This could have shattered me, but I returned briefly to counselling. There I decided that this marriage breakup was not going to be a negative force in my life. I happened to marry someone who himself was hung up sexually and when combined with my sexual discomfort, this led to an unfortunate and painful divorce.

STICKING WITH IT

I married another man who was kind, thoughtful, and sexually patient with me. Eventually I grew more comfortable with intimate contact and began to enjoy our sexual relationship.

SLIPPING BACK

I remind myself of the wonderful life I have ahead of me and how understanding my husband has been.

ADVICE FOR OTHERS

Be cautious rather than free spirited with men. This doesn't mean that you have to be paranoid, but be watchful and slow-moving in your relationships.

Counselling was a lifesaver and I recommend it when you've gone through this kind of trauma. Realize that no matter how bad the assault was, once you put your mind to it, you can place it behind you. That doesn't mean everything will be forgotten, but it just won't interfere in piecing your life back together.

86: MENOPAUSE

Female, Age 58, Furniture Designer

ADVERSITY

I had tremendous difficulties coping with my menopausal symptoms, which included frequent hot flushes, profuse perspiration, frequent mood changes, irritability, and depression. My symptoms were so bad that I cancelled social engagements, tended to withdraw from people, and stayed home more frequently. Often I was tired and irritable and would get most impatient with my daughter. My husband was not understanding or supportive, which ultimately led to some serious marital problems.

SELF-DEFEATING THINKING

Having come from a very traditional European background, I did not have too much knowledge of women's health issues. I did not have any idea what menopause was about, so of course I thought the worst. Because of my ignorance, I thought there was something wrong with me physically. For a while I believed that I might be dying. Because I was not in the habit of seeing doctors, I shied away from them at first. However, my menstrual periods were so irregular and I became so worried, that I decided to make an appointment.

NEW THINKING

I finally saw my family doctor and was reassured that my symptoms were a normal part of the cycle of menopause. This "change of life" that I was experiencing brought with it many fluctuations in hormone levels, so the hot flushes, perspiration, and mood changes were the outcomes.

Also, I recognized that thinking the worst kept me away from my doctor. Had I not believed that I was dying, I would have made an appointment much earlier. Thinking the worst certainly didn't help me, but prevented me from getting advice and counsel much sooner.

EMOTIONAL RESPONSE

There was a tremendous sense of relief. Worry was no longer part of my daily life. In fact, I had worried unnecessarily. This experience taught me to seek out information first before I come to any conclusions, especially negative ones.

SOLUTION AND OUTCOME

I was now able to accept my symptoms more readily and managed to keep myself very busy at work and at home with sewing and socializing. The people whom I had previously avoided were once again part of my social life.

STICKING WITH IT

Increasing my involvement with friends and relatives has helped considerably. I am now able to joke about the mess that I got myself into.

SLIPPING BACK

I don't slip into my old ways because I am no longer bothered by my symptoms. But I am careful not to delay getting help for myself if I need it.

ADVICE FOR OTHERS

Seek professional advice as soon as possible to avoid unnecessary worries. Also, maintain your social contacts and do not avoid engagements. It is important to keep your friends close to you, so that you may share your thoughts, feelings, and fears with them.

87: A PROLONGED HOSPITAL STAY

Female, Age 62, Public Health Professional

ADVERSITY

In the past I had back surgery, which during the healing process caused considerable scar tissue. For a number of years, I was free of back pain, but I was informed that the scarring could, in the future, cause a flare-up. One evening, there was a sudden onset of severe pain in my back and legs. I was immediately rushed to hospital in an ambulance and when I arrived I was injected with Demerol (a pain killer) and immediately confined to bed. Little did I know that I was to remain there for over three months. The next week was a series of Demerol injections, medical consultations, and visits from my husband and three older children. It was decided by the specialist in charge that surgery to remove the scar tissue would be required. The procedure took eight hours. After the surgery, I was flat on my back for two weeks and was given narcotics by nurses who would also turn me every couple of hours. By the third week, I was sitting up in the bed then in a chair. During the fourth week, I began to hobble around in the corridors, but with considerable help.

Because my job as a public health professional involved a great deal of movement in and out of cars and in and out of patients' houses, I eventually had to resign my position, knowing that my back could not tolerate all of the strain. This was a tremendous blow to me because I truly enjoyed what I was doing.

For the next couple of months, the burden of care for the three teenagers fell upon my husband who managed reasonably well under the circumstances. Although my husband and children continued to visit me, my friends came by less often. More and more I began to rely on the hospital staff for support and encouragement.

SELF-DEFEATING THINKING

I constantly worried about having a permanent disability and the prospects seemed real. Would I ever work again? How would my family handle a

196

"cripple"? Would I ever resume a normal life? What would happen to me in the future? How would I ever get through another painful day in this hospital? The same routine day in and day out was driving me crazy. Also, I was taking narcotics and worried about developing an addiction to these drugs that I had been taking for a while. My life at the hospital was filled with hopelessness, helplessness, and depression. Because of my miserable state, I was referred to a psychiatrist who presumably was going to deal with all of my concerns.

NEW THINKING

My psychiatrist had no sensitivity whatsoever. I thought his ideas were full of shit. It was then that I decided I could help myself more. This was my turning point. I would do everything on my own. My determination would help me to walk again. With continued and persistent practice, I gradually started to walk again, although it was a slow process. Occasionally I would scream at myself, "Well damn it, I'm going to get better no matter what!" It was clear that I wanted to get better for me, not for my family, not for my doctors, not for my friends, but for me. I wanted and got control of my health and my life. It sounds selfish, but it wasn't meant that way. I simply focused all my energies on me.

EMOTIONAL RESPONSE

I felt tremendous satisfaction in being able to cope with my physical problem and my long rehabilitation in the hospital. To say that I was proud of myself is putting it mildly. I actually overcame my own depression—that's an accomplishment!

SOLUTION AND OUTCOME

Prior to my hospitalization, I had always done things because they were "right" to do. What would people say if I broke with tradition? So I always did what was expected of me. It was going to be different now, because I was different, not only physically, but more important, psychologically. My needs would now take priority. If I couldn't run up the stairs, I would walk. If I didn't feel like going somewhere, I would say no. If my family wanted a meal and I wasn't up to preparing it, they would get their own meals or they could order food in.

STICKING WITH IT

I do more things now just to prove that I can do them for myself. Difficult tasks are challenges to test my resources. In the past I would back away from something that might cause my back pain, now I go after what life has to offer me.

SLIPPING BACK

When I feel defeated about a situation, my thinking eventually comes around to how I plan to overcome this and then I repeat to myself, "I am not going to let this beat me." I defy my problem. I get buoyant to the point where I know I will handle this situation somehow. I realize that in overcoming my painful problem and my long hospital stay, I developed a strong mental capability. I now believe in myself more than ever before and I know that this profound change in my thinking will remain with me.

ADVICE FOR OTHERS

Don't give up until you're dead! You can repeat all of the old cliches, for example, "It's going to get better tomorrow." Some people give in gracefully and accept adversity and don't fight back like I did. The answer for me has been fight it, challenge it, and overcome it—and then stand up and say I have done it. That is my message to you.

88: AGING

Male, Age 69, Writer

ADVERSITY

I am not sure which adversity you mean. Life is a constant challenge and the secret is, of course, to cope with the many challenges. However, the latest was tension or stress due solely to aging. I was grappling with a slowing down of my physical abilities. Aches and pains, which I had never experienced before, seemed to be in every bone of my body. My strength, upon which I had counted all of my life, seemed to be lessening. Some mornings, I would find it difficult crawling out of bed. That simply was not like me.

SELF-DEFEATING THINKING

How could this happen to me? Here my body was failing me, would my mind be next? Everything that I had ever feared about aging came to the fore. My anxiety level was so high that I ran to my family doctor.

NEW THINKING

After a thorough examination, I was told that my body was not failing me, but my mind was working overtime. It had become obvious that the normal process of aging carries with it the baggage of unusual and unpredictable aches. It was now my job to accept this!

EMOTIONAL RESPONSE

I was disappointed and at the same time relieved. Had I known that this was going to happen to my body, I would have stayed young forever.

SOLUTION AND OUTCOME

No longer did I allow myself the agony of worry. If my body was showing signs of wear and tear more one day than the next, so be it.

STICKING WITH IT

My outlook has always been to exercise common sense and courage. I certainly have exercised considerably more common sense lately.

SLIPPING BACK

It's what I don't do that is important. I no longer linger in self-pity and fear about what might happen to me in the future. The side effects of aging are now an acceptable part of this ongoing process.

ADVICE FOR OTHERS

The secret of longevity is mobility, to remain curious and to exercise your imagination.

89: STARTING OVER

Female, Age 69, Hospital Volunteer Coordinator

ADVERSITY

My husband had a blocked aortic valve and needed surgery. He was rushed to hospital, but insisted on being discharged to attend his daughter's wedding. After the wedding, he was readmitted and scheduled for surgery within a couple of days. My husband died three days after he was operated on.

Devastation was my immediate reaction. I did not anticipate that he would die. The support from my family did not materialize. It seemed like one disappointment after another. Then there was my sister's wedding, which was arranged well before the surgery and which I was expected to attend. My sister couldn't understand that I would have extreme difficulty dealing with this festive occasion. The last thing I needed was to celebrate her remarriage. A few weeks passed and it was then I decided that I needed to start over. I left the city and moved to a larger one.

Slowly I lost contact with my old friends and relatives. My new circle of friends, many of whom were widowed, were actually more supportive. It was apparent that my family and friends back home were unable to handle my grief and suffering.

Now I was faced with what to do with my time and energy.

SELF-DEFEATING THINKING

At first I could not decide what direction to take. I was stuck. Paralyzed was more like it. Questions kept popping up in my head: "What do I want to do?" "What's the right thing for me to do?" Failure was truly what worried me the most. Taking a chance on something meant the risk of not succeeding. After all I had been through, the last thing I needed was to do poorly at something.

NEW THINKING

I had been through so much and handled it well, why was I doing this to myself now. I took hold of myself and said, "I'm responsible for my own destiny and must accept bad things in life along with the good things." I knew that there was a risk of failure no matter what I did. But I guess I wanted to be "sure," but what indeed is "sure" in life. And certainly I knew the answer to that. So I put on my hat and coat and went out there and made contact with the world.

EMOTIONAL RESPONSE

Once I started to focus on controlling my life, I felt uplifted.

SOLUTION AND OUTCOME

I spoke to a number of volunteer organizations and discovered that hospitals were in desperate need of dedicated people who wanted to make an important contribution. This was what I wanted, a chance to be a useful member of society.

STICKING WITH IT

I cultivated a strong support group of single and widowed friends, as well as fellow volunteers, who have been a great source of strength for me.

SLIPPING BACK

What I have accomplished over such a short period of time is a welcome reminder when I start feeling sorry for myself. I truly did start over and that will never be forgotten.

ADVICE FOR OTHERS

You cannot change the bad things that happen to you, but you can change how you deal with your reactions to them. If you have to make a drastic change in your lifestyle, ask yourself what you really want to do. When you have your answer then go about making the changes that are necessary to reach your goal. You are responsible for your destiny and until you accept that responsibility and take control of your life you will continue to be caught in the past and never finish grieving. Then put on your hat and coat and make contact!

90: TAKING AN EXAMINATION

Male, Age 37 Laboratory Technician

ADVERSITY

My father was a perfectionist and this may have contributed to my problem. I would literally become physically ill in high school prior to exams.

As a young boy, as far back as I can remember, I always strove to be the best. I was and still am a perfectionist and highly competitive. To make my parents proud of me was a burning desire. They were proud I'm sure, but I never really felt I accomplished enough. Long hours would be spent studying even though I knew the material. I would read it over just one more time to make sure and then worry endlessly and needlessly about failing, which I knew would not happen—but I got myself physically ill stewing about it. I was embarrassed and ashamed of this behavior and knew that my parents would never have approved, so I kept it well hidden. Because my priority was to do as well as possible, studying, reading, and working on papers and projects occupied most of my time, which meant there was virtually no opportunity to create and maintain friendships. So I had few acquaintances, because my world revolved around doing well in school.

Sometimes I really envied people who took life more easily and freely. They didn't seem to have the same cares and worries about being perfect and doing well on exams and tests. Yet I was so hard on myself and so demanding.

SELF-DEFEATING THINKING

Thinking about failure and how embarrassed I and my family would be. Even though I knew in my heart I would do well, in my head, I thought otherwise. What a vicious circle! I would get upset and worry, study excessively, feel ill before writing an exam, and yet do really well. But I didn't want to change this crazy pattern, because it seemed to work.

NEW THINKING

A friend, with whom I had grown up, one day came out and said, "Smarten up. Why worry about things that have happened or may never happen? Save your energy for important matters." This really hit home, the notion of expending my energy on important issues, not on worry. There was no reason for me to behave the way I used to. An exam only reflects perhaps two hours in my life. There was no reason to get so upset. This didn't mean that I had to ease up on my ambitions, but simply cut out all the anxiety and sick feelings that I created.

EMOTIONAL RESPONSE

I stopped being as nervous and felt more in control. After all, it was just an examination, which I can handle and have handled.

SOLUTION AND OUTCOME

It was noticeable to me and to others that I had become more settled and even-tempered. People even said that I was more relaxed. I'm now able to think more logically about situations and put "a cap" on my perfectionism and realize through conscious effort that being number one isn't always what counts, it's trying that counts.

STICKING WITH IT

Maturity of thought and constant reminders from myself and others have done it for me. But mainly it is my mind set. Life is too short to go on the way I used to. To date, I have fortunately done well on all of the exams I have taken and I hope that will continue, but I refuse to drive myself crazy about what the future holds.

SLIPPING BACK

Recently there were certification exams that I was required to take, and I noticed that I was becoming lightheaded. Before writing my first exam, I went for a walk, took a deep breath, and started talking to myself. This was merely a written test that required my best effort and only my best effort, I repeated. I continued to walk until I talked myself down. Then I went into the examination room and wrote the test with little anxiety.

ADVICE FOR OTHERS

People should look at all they have accomplished, both big and small. Write a list of your successes and celebrate them. Even writing down your thoughts can make them more logical, and eventually lead to problem resolution. Practice makes perfect. The more you take exams, the better you should become. Talk yourself into the proper frame of mind, and remind yourself that you can do it without all of that worry. Finally, discuss your concerns with others, as you may find that you're not alone and sometimes this can make a difference.

91: DISCOVERING YOU ARE ADOPTED

Female, Age 62, Entrepreneur

ADVERSITY

Early in my career, when I was engaged to be married, I went with my fiancee and older sister to buy an engagement ring. Because he didn't have enough money, he had borrowed it from my sister. When I found this out, I was so upset that I gave the ring to my sister who, in essence, had paid for it. She, in turn, was very annoyed with me for wanting to break off the engagement and told me virtually to get out of our house. Being 17 years old then and given that my parents were retired, she ruled the house. In a rage, she barked out that I was adopted and this was not really my home.

I did leave the house and went to stay with some close friends who were very supportive and encouraging. I was devastated, disappointed, and extremely bitter. When I spoke to my parents to verify what my sister had said, they indeed stated it was true.

After that I never returned home. Stubbornness prevented me from going back. I didn't want to live with my dominating, destructive sister who had always treated me poorly. My parents always showed me a great deal of love and attention and didn't treat me any differently than my older sister. Yet I ceased to maintain contact with them, and they in turn failed to keep in touch with me.

SELF-DEFEATING THINKING

Maybe my parents didn't care for me after all. Why was I abandoned? Wasn't anyone interested in my welfare? I literally thought that the world had given up on me.

NEW THINKING

Because I am a strong and determined person, I refused to let this experience break me. Although I had considerable animosity towards my sister, I knew deep down that my parents did love me and had shown no malice towards me. In turn I had no misgivings about my parents. They were now elderly and heavily relied upon my older sister to look after them.

EMOTIONAL RESPONSE

I felt sorry for my parents. It was a shame that our relationship had taken a turn for the worse, but clearly my sister had instigated it and was probably pleased that things were this way.

Now I began to wonder who my real parents were. If only there were pictures. So many questions remained unanswered.

SOLUTION AND OUTCOME

I never did follow through to find out who my real parents were, because I married a wonderful man to whom I devoted myself. Never did I look back, because there was too much to look forward to.

STICKING WITH IT

By not thinking about it. If an incident comes up and throws me back, I have my husband's support. We truly have a strong relationship, which is a great source of strength in my life.

SLIPPING BACK

There was a major slip, when I received a measly postcard from my sister, to inform me of my mother's death some three months later. I was hysterical, angry, crying, but with the support of my father-in-law and my husband, I realized there was nothing I could do or gain from extreme hatred. However, it took me awhile to get over that one.

ADVICE FOR OTHERS

It's not the end of the world! Get on with your life. But remember the people who adopted you, you owe them something; they loved you for a long time.

92: GOING TO THE DENTIST

Male, Age 52, Chemical Engineer

ADVERSITY

I was not taken to the dentist until I was seven years old, at which time I had a terrible abscess. He was an old-fashioned dentist with antiquated equipment and I required an anaesthetic. It was a very traumatic experience.

Also, I had a "problem mouth" in which the teeth were very crowded and uneven. I was supposed to go back again to have work done to correct these problems, but after several abortive attempts, I never did return.

At the age of about 16 I did go to another dentist who felt that my orthodontic problems were beyond him and he referred me to a dental school where they took out several very decayed teeth. I again did not keep my return appointment because I was scared.

Now as an adult, I have gone to the dentist, but my tension level increases dramatically as the event approaches. My family members have dealt with this in the past by poking fun at me, so now I don't tell them when my appointments are.

SELF-DEFEATING THINKING

Why am I putting myself through this trauma and pain? If my teeth were a little crooked and I had no discomfort, there was no reason to go to the dentist. I hated losing control while under anaesthetic and hated to hear all of those sounds from the apparatus.

NEW THINKING

There was an overriding thought that always came to mind, but I didn't know where it originated. That is, I have to get my teeth fixed and keep them fixed no matter what. If there was dental pain, I would have to endure it.

EMOTIONAL RESPONSE

After every appointment I kept, I felt good about the dental work that was completed. Yet prior to the next appointment, the butterflies in my stomach spread their wings again and began to fly!

SOLUTION AND OUTCOME

I simply pushed myself and knew that I must endure the discomfort to keep a healthy mouth.

STICKING WITH IT

Recently, when a filling fell out, I remembered thinking that I had better get it replaced or all my efforts would be worthless. The consequences were more serious if I didn't get it fixed. I couldn't let all the work done now be ruined by decay.

SLIPPING BACK

I will still occasionally procrastinate if left to my own devices. Right now, I'm supposed to make arrangements for a root canal. I know I will eventually get it done when the time is right.

I try to avoid having to make my own dental appointments, because it is hard for me. My regular dentist is understanding of my fear and his office books a recall appointment every six months. Once the appointment is made, I keep it.

ADVICE FOR OTHERS

Find a dentist who is sympathetic to your fears. Make up your mind that you have to do it and do it! Remind yourself that the more frequently you go routinely, the less likely the dentist will find problems. Choose a good time frame for yourself. Early in the morning when there are fewer distractions is best for me. Have your dentist prearrange your appointments if that is helpful. Keep your anxiety to yourself if you find people make fun of your fear of going to the dentist.

93: FEELING UNATTRACTIVE

Female, Age 29, Marketing Assistant

ADVERSITY

I was never a skinny child and I also like to eat.

As an adult, I really enjoyed good cooking then I found I was eating anything that resembled food. In a short period of time, I had put on 40 lbs and I was feeling like a fat ugly slob.

Most of my friends looked attractive and slim, yet my dress sizes kept jumping and my closet was getting crowded with old clothes that I'd never wear. More and more I became a real homebody refusing to go out. There was nothing to wear and those things that did fit, made me look dumpy.

Living at home with my parents, I noticed that they would avoid subjects that they thought would upset me. They never mentioned running into any of my friends. My mother made excuses for my failure to socialize. Although I felt guilty that she was doing this for me, at the same time I was grateful. It was like being a kid again and mummy was making things "all better," except that it wasn't.

Slowly my friends drifted, because they got tired of my no-shows. After a while I got really angry at my family for letting me just get uglier and uglier. I was moody and difficult to live with and I don't know how my parents put up with me, but they stuck by me. Like any other family, they felt it was their duty.

At work, I felt more unattractive than anywhere else, because I was surrounded by slim, good-looking peers. So my mood swings were unpredictable. People would ask me how I was feeling that day and depending on the answer, they'd either join me for coffee or lunch or they would avoid me altogether. At times, I guess I was a real bitch. It wasn't so much the weight that bothered me, as this overpowering feeling that I was really unattractive.

SELF-DEFEATING THINKING

I rationalized that I could never do anything about it so why bother. I'd always been ugly and fat and history can't be changed overnight. But I hated myself this way. Unconsciously, I found myself hanging around heavier, sloppy people to take some of the attention away from me.

NEW THINKING

If you dislike something enough, it can motivate you to try something different. I guess it was the fact that I was turning 30 and was thoroughly fed up with being fat and ugly. My friends from college were all married and seemed to be happy, and here I was single and probably destined to stay that way. Is this the way I wanted to spend the rest of my life and if not what was I going to do about it? I was totally committed to trying to change.

EMOTIONAL RESPONSE

I felt driven. This was my opportunity to make a difference in my life. I began to research programs and services that could help me.

SOLUTION AND OUTCOME

I enrolled in a program that taught me how to use make-up effectively, entered a weight reduction program, and signed up for dancing lessons. Then I started to go out more often with new people and resumed a lot of my old friendships. Instead of avoiding social contacts, I'd agree to go out and do almost anything. I even found myself agreeing to have photos taken of myself, which I used to hate.

STICKING WITH IT

I've become more physically active, working out four or five times a week. Now I find myself advising others on how to improve their own lifestyles. I have an old photo of myself when I was ugly and fat, stuck on my refrigerator to remind me never to be that way again.

SLIPPING BACK

I phone up close friends and talk to them. Also, I keep a few old baggy dresses in the closet that act as a powerful reminder of how I used to be and never again want to become. I feel too good about myself to let things slide.

ADVICE FOR OTHERS

Whatever it is that bothers you, whether it's your weight, your appearance, your physical conditioning, you need to commit yourself to change, not for anyone else but for yourself. Work at change slowly, because that way you get used to the gradual differences. Set small realistic goals and then reward yourself when you reach each one. I'm certain this can work for anyone who is dedicated to self-improvement.

94: LOSING EYESIGHT

Female, Age 73, Senior Citizen

ADVERSITY

I am virtually blind in my left eye. One year ago, I had a cataract removed and a lens implant, and was seeing as clear as could be. Then during a check-up three months later, the doctor said there was some scarring on the back of this eye, and wanted to see me again in three months. My vision in the left eye was being blocked out in the center, and I could only see out of the corner of the eye. During the next visit, I failed the many visual tests that the technician administered. The doctor said that the scar tissue in the back of my eye was clearly hurting my vision and there was virtually nothing that could be done. It was also advised that the cataract in my right eye be left alone in the hope that it wouldn't get worse. The doctor assured me that it hadn't grown since the previous year.

This affected my personal life because now, in addition to a right hand that was crippled with arthritis and hard to use, I literally couldn't see out of my left eye. I had to concentrate twice as hard to do any task that once was easy. When I walked, I staggered slightly to the left. Once, leaving a department store with a neighbor, another woman commented to her friend how disgusting it was to see a woman of my age drunk. This really upset my neighbor, and it made me angry and embarrassed. For a week I worried that my neighbor would not want to be seen with me again. I finally asked her, and she reassured me she thought no such thing.

It was difficult to take the bus, especially on those days when family or neighbors were not available to assist me. I was terrified of crossing the street, as the drivers today don't stop for anybody. At times I would swear out of frustration, which I never did before. I also had to look after my husband, which meant carting his meals up a flight of stairs to his room when he wasn't feeling well, and lately, that was often. The most troublesome matter for me was that I was more dependent on my family and friends, but they loved me and tried to help out as much as they could.

SELF-DEFEATING THINKING

I was upset and distraught at times. I feared that I might lose my total vision. That terrified me. Total darkness, no sky, no sunshine, no sunset. To me, the world was full of beauty to see. To be without sight would be an awful thing.

I had never had a lot of patience, and I found that now I was frustrating myself more often. The simplest task became difficult, not only because of my failing vision but also there was no feeling and little strength in my right hand. Everything I did felt off balance. I was angry at the doctor. I thought maybe the resident who performed the surgery had made a mistake. Had the surgery not taken place, I might still have some vision in my left eye.

NEW THINKING

I decided to lock those feelings of frustration away, otherwise they would control me, and bring me down. When I can't do what I used to do, I will try harder. It might take me longer or I might have to do it differently, but I would persevere. I must accept my loss and go on. I've always had a philosophy that what I can't change I've got to learn to live with and this would be more important now then ever before.

EMOTIONAL RESPONSE

Once I accepted my vision wasn't going to get better, I felt that there was a major challenge before me. I couldn't give up. I felt a little better that I had accepted the inevitable and could go on.

SOLUTION AND OUTCOME

When I am clumsy, I still get frustrated, but my determination does not cease.

STICKING WITH IT

I keep trying; I'm determined to do the best I can. This has always been part of my nature.

SLIPPING BACK

I find something to do that takes effort or concentration. I work it out of my system, like doing some chores.

The worst thing you can do is believe there is nothing left in life and wait in a corner for someone to do everything for you. No matter how many mistakes you make, or how many things you drop, or how hard it is to find things, you must keep trying!

95: GETTING IN TROUBLE WITH THE LAW

Male, Age 25, Loader/Shipper

ADVERSITY

I was involved with drugs and other illegal activities. I was in court three times; the first and second time for possession of marijuana, the third time for dealing cocaine. After attending a treatment center for two days, I found that none of their methods could help me, and I resolved to change my ways on my own.

My involvement with drugs started when I was 15, by associating with a "bad crowd" of friends. I quit school, quit my job, and supported myself through dealing drugs. The money that I obtained only served to support my own drug habit. When I was finally arrested for the first time, I could have ended up in jail, but because I had no prior convictions, I was released. At this point, I was also living off the avails of assault, extortion, and prostitution.

When my mother found out, she was really shocked. But she was still supportive and at least I had a place to stay. My younger sister didn't understand what was happening to me, and she simply observed me as I went through my "stages of regression." My older brother acted as my father figure in the absence of my real father, as my parents were divorced.

He always wanted to talk to me, but I ignored him. Because I had quit my job, I often found myself in a tight squeeze for money. The third time I was arrested for possession of cocaine, I thought for sure that I'd spend six to eight months in jail. However, my brother helped me with $3,500 for a good criminal lawyer.

SELF-DEFEATING THINKING

At that time, I was so confused and so angry. My parents had separated when I was ten, and it really affected me. I had good friends throughout my early teenage years, but the bad company took over and I turned to drugs. At 16, it was like something inside me snapped and my attitude was "to hell with everybody." It was my bad attitude and all my pent-up frustrations that kept me in this mess.

NEW THINKING

I was almost 20 at this time. My friend was in the same situation as I was, and he wanted to change. He said to me that I wasn't the same guy he had met five years ago, and that I was killing myself, slowly but surely. I knew that he had a point, and that I should straighten out my life before I ended up doing myself in from the use of drugs, or permanently ended up in jail. When my brother helped me financially to stay out of jail, I knew that I had to change my ways or I would end up dead one of these days. In other words, I valued my life enough that I wanted to go on living.

EMOTIONAL RESPONSE

I suddenly realized that in my five years, I had done more booze, more drugs, and more things to my life and to my family than a lot of people could do in one lifetime! Suddenly I felt that my life was not worth throwing away but indeed was worth something.

SOLUTION AND OUTCOME

I eventually got a job in a factory, which kept me busy for eight to ten hours of the day, and it helped me feel that I was accomplishing something, and getting my life back on track. I went through my mood swings of being depressed one day, and happy the next, but keeping busy helped to keep me out of trouble with the law. It also gave me a sense of security. My family was ecstatic that I was holding down a job.

STICKING WITH IT

I write letters to myself constantly, summarizing what I've experienced. By rereading them, I realized that at first I was a confused young man and now my life has literally turned around. There is money in the bank, I have investments, I have a good job, I have a great outlook. But most of all, I have a family who supported me and never kicked me out of the house—they were always there for me.

SLIPPING BACK

When I see myself starting to slip, I don't allow myself to go back to my old habits and lifestyle. I have been in trouble with the law enough times to know that the old way is the wrong way. As a recovering drug addict/alcoholic, I will always have this temptation to try a joint or a shot, but instead I concentrate on the good things about my new lifestyle.

ADVICE FOR OTHERS

The best advice for people who have the same problem is that you have to want to help yourself before you can change. I've been through it, so I know what it is like. For people who have never been involved seriously with the law, the best thing, of course, is to avoid getting into illegal situations. Proper education concerning drugs and the effect of alcohol is important. Today the media don't glorify drugs and students are better informed about the dangers. Also, realize as a drug addict/alcoholic that you are never completely cured, so that you have to remain vigilant for your entire life.

96: POOR MEMORY

Female, Age 48, Manager of a Health Center

ADVERSITY

My sister and her husband had migrated to Australia leaving me in their house with her two children and our mother who had severe rheumatoid arthritis. They returned to stay in the same house with us. Her husband at this time was suffering from a nervous breakdown, and was very depressed. I was scheduled to take a very important management course that was considered essential to the operation of the health center, but I opted to postpone it until matters had settled at home. The management board was especially disturbed that I had chosen to delay taking this critical program, yet I refused to tell them the turmoil I was going through at home. Then suddenly my sister decided to sell the house and move out to the West End, which was further away from my work, but I had no choice so I moved in with them, which in hindsight was a mistake. By this time my mother's arthritis was getting worse and she was now bedridden. I was trying to cope the best way I could, when my brother was diagnosed with leukemia. I needed to take time off from work, but I wasn't able to without having to worry about my assistant whom I discovered was a drug addict.

Then it happened. My memory went. I couldn't recall what projects were going on at work. Colleagues' names were forgotten. On a number of occasions, I got lost driving home. At important meetings, I would sound incoherent. The last straw was the time I forgot my own name when I was introducing myself to an important political figure.

SELF-DEFEATING THINKING

I was burdened with the thought that I either had a brain tumor or was headed for a nervous breakdown. I had prided myself on my ability to retain and recall information at will, yet my memory was now failing me badly. What would I do if I couldn't think clearly anymore? Would I turn into a "human vegetable"? I'd rather die than not know what I was doing!

NEW THINKING

"Stay calm," was what I repeated to myself. My irrational thoughts were running away with my mind. At this point, I needed to obtain more information about what was wrong with me and thus needed to seek out the opinion of a professional.

EMOTIONAL RESPONSE

Scared shitless! But also I felt more settled that I was finally doing something to help myself rather than drive myself nutty by worrying.

SOLUTION AND OUTCOME

After coming out of my family doctor's office, it all fell into place. Because of my heightened anxiety about all that was going on in my life, I was confused to the point where I was forgetting. Because there were too many balls being juggled at the same time, my mind couldn't effectively process all the information coming at me. I also came to the conclusion that I needed to look after myself better. Clearly *I* had not been a priority in my life. So I moved away from my family, by renting a condominium closer to my health center. I referred my assistant to a treatment center. My board was informed of the personal turmoil I was experiencing and were told that I would enroll in that important course in about three months. Then I called up a few close friends and started to go out for the first in a long time.

STICKING WITH IT

I tell myself that this is a healthier way to live and I am dedicated to maintaining it. Unnecessary stressors are removed or changed. By the way, my memory has been great! I feel like a whole person again.

SLIPPING BACK

I haven't slipped into my old ways yet and do not plan to.

ADVICE FOR OTHERS

You should not feel obligated to do something just because it is expected of you. Once your mind is overloaded, your memory can indeed suffer. Know when enough is enough. Seek professional help if you need guidance. A forgetful mind can often be a sign that you are indeed overdoing it.

Don't think that you are selfish if you put yourself first, before the demands of others.

97: MOVING AWAY TO COLLEGE

Male, Age 21, Medical Student

ADVERSITY

I had worked so hard throughout my high-school years. My dream was to get a high enough average so that I could go to the college of my choice. Well, I chose to go out of town to a science program that was considered to be one of the best in the country. I arrived with all of the enthusiasm in the world. Although I had never been away from home before, I thought that I could easily handle it. But it really wasn't that easy after all. Suddenly, I was faced with many new people and the pressure to establish new relationships. My traditional securities and supports no longer surrounded me. I truly was on my own and was beginning to dislike it.

SELF-DEFEATING THINKING

I couldn't stand this sudden, intense loneliness. My close friends were no longer part of my life, and neither was my family. Who was I going to talk to? All these new strangers seemed so intimidating. Then I began to run myself down. Boy, was I a wimp. An insecure, awkward, and foolish guy who couldn't stand up on his own two feet. At this point I thought that I was going to run away and leave everything behind me. But where would I go? People back home would really think that I was a baby, who couldn't stay away from his mommy and daddy.

NEW THINKING

My personal breakthrough came when I spoke to a couple of other students who came right out and told me how lonely and intimidated they were. I was not alone and I could share what I was feeling with these people, who were now becoming good friends.

Maturity is being able to understand what you are going through and have the courage to talk about it and not necessarily judge it. I guess that I had finally matured.

EMOTIONAL RESPONSE

I felt considerably more comfortable and was excited about the new relationships I was forming. I no longer felt driven to run away because this was where I belonged. No longer did I have the urge to return home to the security of family and old friends. Any regrets that I previously had about going away to college had disappeared.

SOLUTION AND OUTCOME

My friendships suddenly grew in number. Also, when I spoke to family back home, I was able to relate what I had been through and how I was now managing. There were a number of college committees that I joined, and I began to direct my energies to enjoying the campus lifestyle rather than to returning home.

STICKING WITH IT

I keep extremely busy with my schoolwork, my friendships, and my campus activities. I maintain a strong, positive outlook and remind myself of my career goals and the profession that I want to pursue.

SLIPPING BACK

I remind myself of all that has happened and how I managed to get through it. My friendships are great sources of support. In fact, we have weekly rap sessions to get caught up with what one another is doing and how we are feeling. Also, I look forward to what lies ahead with greater enthusiasm.

ADVICE FOR OTHERS

Accept change, don't fight it. Later on you will have to accept a great deal more change and responsibility, especially when you enter the work world, so you might as well begin the process now.

Accept that there will be lonely times and that it is quite normal. Finally, trust in your ability to make new friends.

98: EXPERIENCING PREJUDICE

Female, Age 39, Theater Director

ADVERSITY

I always disagreed with my father from early childhood on such matters as religion, racism, and tolerance of others. We were on opposite sides of every discussion. He imposed his will on me to the point where he split up my relationship with my boyfriend and prevented me from eventually marrying this man.

Because of this controversy, I moved away from home and remained unmarried for a considerable number of years. Every subsequent boyfriend met with complete disapproval from my father. Finally, I met the man of my dreams, but it just so happened that he was black. To alleviate possible tensions, I purposely kept my future husband's family and my family apart until the wedding day. Just prior to the wedding day, I received two telephone calls. The first was from my father who swore at me over the phone and shouted that I was "fornicating with a nigger." Furthermore, he said that I was never to return home. In essence, he had disowned me and made it clear that I would not be accepted by any part of society.

The next call was from my future father-in-law who plainly declared that,

"We don't want a 'whitey' in the family." I was appalled at both families. Never before had I personally experienced prejudice. For a period of time, I withdrew from my future husband and refused to tell him what had transpired because I wasn't sure what his reaction might be. To jeopardize our wedding and marriage was a grave fear of mine. However, my sister and brother and my future brothers-in-law came to my aid. They knew what had happened and tried to be as considerate as possible. Also, they went back to their respective parents and fought to defend my position, but to no avail. When my future husband and I did discuss what had transpired, we became more committed to one another than ever before. But the whole affair was nonetheless very disturbing.

In fact, one evening at the theater, I began to experience an odd numbness down my left side and was convinced that I was about to have a heart attack. In the emergency room of the hospital, I discovered that it was merely my nerves.

At work, my friends and associates were most understanding. We discussed at great length the impact that prejudice and racism can have, especially on a new marriage. No doubt, my future husband and I would need to have a strong bond to guard ourselves against the prejudicial onslaught coming from both families.

SELF-DEFEATING THINKING

In reviewing my life at home with a domineering and intimidating father, I realized how much I despised him. What right did he ever have to tell me whom I would or would not marry? He had no right to treat me with such disrespect and disregard for my feelings. My mother was no better because she went along with him. My home life was a series of interferences and much harassment, which I would never forget. As for my future father-in-law, he didn't seem to be that much better. Who did he think he was calling me and making those prejudicial slurs.

NEW THINKING

With considerable help from my future husband, my aunt, my sister and brother, friends, and colleagues, I was able to step forward and dismiss both my father's and father-in-law's prejudices. Both of these men had serious faults and shortcomings. Their upbringing I'm sure had a great deal to do with shaping their present beliefs and behaviors. I no longer felt less of a person because of their harsh judgments. They were entitled to their racist opinions, but in no way would I allow their prejudices to interfere with my wedding plans and my marital relationship. My future husband and I would not be dragged down to their level.

EMOTIONAL RESPONSE

I felt rejuvenated and had regained my self-respect. Also, I was proud of my ability to step back and objectively evaluate what was said about me rather than take it very personally and wallow in self-pity.

SOLUTION AND OUTCOME

To begin with, we had a great wedding, although neither set of parents was in attendance. My husband and I truly are committed to having a wonderful life together. No longer would my father interfere in my life! I do not confide in my parents nor do I value their opinions. On occasion, I visit them—without my husband, of course—spend more time talking to my brother and sister, then leave.

STICKING WITH IT

I refuse to let anything interfere with my happiness and the love my husband and I have for one another.

SLIPPING BACK

I force myself to stop and think about what I am feeling. Through sheer strength of character, I do not allow others to interfere with my judgment. I don't beat myself up and I don't accept responsibility for anyone else's actions anymore.

ADVICE FOR OTHERS

Do not allow other people to hurt your judgment and your self-respect. Be responsible for your own actions and don't try to change other people. Realize that these adversities can make you a stronger person if you use your best judgment and trust yourself. Be proud of your accomplishments, and do not be controlled by others. Be true to thyself!

99: PROBLEM WITH TRANQUILIZERS

Male, Age 51, Actor

ADVERSITY

That is difficult to do. It depends on whether constantly taking tranquilizers is a problem or a disease. Events leading up to it are life events. Factors in life determine if a person is going to overcome the disease or succumb to it. With me, it was a series of events that made me succumb to the disease. It was my inability to cope with reality, with relationships, which in turn led to the abuse of this prescription drug. One major event was my emigration to Canada, which for the longest time I regretted and had trouble accepting. I simply rejected the society that I was living in. My rejection of Canadian society led me to opt out of college and to go to the arts, which was a rebellion, a dropping out of traditionalism in favor of creating my own little world, my own little society. This brought with it the struggle to earn a living, the rejection by people who didn't understand my inner turmoil, the failure of numerous relationships, my eventual inability to get close to people, and the ultimate addiction to that "blessed pill."

As Valium took over my life, I wanted very little to do with others. My world was one of solitude, selfishness, rudeness, and intolerance. Surprisingly enough my work as an actor was unaffected at first. My work was unhindered and consumed most of my energy and time and focus, until my Valium problem began getting in the way. Then I gave up on everything except those pills. Everything became so difficult, such a chore. My behavior then became unpredictable and my relationships at work began to deteriorate. People were actually afraid of me and began to doubt my judgment. On stage, I blamed them, but inwardly, I knew that I was the culprit, the guilty party—and how painful that was. As my psychological pain increased, so did my intake of tranquilizers. My only escape was that provided by those colorful little "mind benders."

SELF-DEFEATING THINKING

The emotional burden was so heavy that I no longer gave a damn. The pills would wipe everything away and would provide me with the escape hatch that I needed desperately. In fact, these mind-numbing tablets were my constant companion.

NEW THINKING

When I slipped into thinking of my wasted life and thoughts of suicide entered the picture, that's when I knew I had to get help. Someone had to help me sort my life out! I knew I was in trouble, but it was hard to admit it to myself. I realized I was caught in a mess, things were going round and round in my head, but nothing was clear—Where to go? Who to talk to? I ended up in an addiction center. There one of the residents came up to me and told me that I had an addiction. I'm sure that I was an addict, but I didn't want anyone else to tell me. He further told me that he knew what I was going through and where I would be if I continued. This addiction would destroy my health and ruin the emotional health of my parents who had by this time become quite aware of my problem. The truth hit me hard. Then and only then did I realize that I had a disease that required my full attention and a commitment to beat it.

EMOTIONAL RESPONSE

Every single step towards understanding was an achievement, a relief. To attempt to do the smallest thing; to be able to say I was addicted, was a relief! To say anything truthful was a relief! Not to deceive myself was a relief!

SOLUTION AND OUTCOME

It's not an overnight thing, but an extended process of discovery. I have an understanding of who I am and why I am. I discovered that I was alive. Life is the exact opposite of how I used to feel, live, and think. Now I remain constantly aware that I have a problem. When I get angry or frustrated, I do not resort to pills, but rely on my ability to talk myself down and see the bright side.

STICKING WITH IT

I see the positive side and live a life in which I rise above the problem. If I cannot, then I call someone who understands tranquilizer addiction and talk out the problem. Before, I used to pretend that it would go away.

SLIPPING BACK

I keep my weaknesses clearly in mind, and I am not afraid to accept them and talk with someone about them. Also, I look beyond the immediate into a bright future filled with hope and happiness.

ADVICE FOR OTHERS

Live life in the here and now. Keep self and heart open to others. Don't close yourself off. Look for the good things in people. Confess faults, bad thoughts, too. Have humility, and above all, self-respect.

THE PERSONAL SOLUTION

Minds racing, palms sweating, hearts pounding, blood pressure rising, performance slipping—these are common stress reactions to the many unpredictable changes that we experience over the course of our lifetimes. Sadly enough, most of us haven't learned much about stress management, but we talk ourselves into "quick fixes" that have no lasting benefits.

In our pursuit of immediate gratification—a big house, two cars in the garage, the best job, car phones, personal computers, designer clothes, compact disk players—we are burning out. There are more people today than ever before who are asking themselves, "Is that all there is?" After we have busted our butts to achieve all of these material goals, we must question the real worth of these objectives. Are they worth the high price we pay in terms of health and happiness?

In our attempt to push ahead, fulfill our ambitions, and strive for success, we find ourselves frustrated more easily. Anger and annoyance follow us everywhere because others always seem "to get in the way." As we hurriedly drive down the busy streets during rush hour to get to our destinations, we yell, we shout, we scream, we curse, we pound our fists. No wonder we have resorted to using weapons to get our message across. If we simply eliminate others who stand in our way, we will surely reach our destination on time.

Not only have we resorted to weapons to shoot down the opposition, but we have also resorted to drugs to enhance our own capabilities. Cocaine, "ice," steroids, the list goes on and on. People have to get that edge on everyone else. People have to outperform one another.

After we psychologically destroy ourselves, and then realize that it wasn't worth it, we begin to ask ourselves who we truly are and what life is really all about. Very disoriented and confused, we begin to search for alternate lifestyles. As a result, cults of every type have grabbed the attention of many people in our society. These groups offer an alternative to the frenzied, frenetic pace that is required to replicate "the lives of the rich and famous." Once inculcated, once brainwashed with the powerful views of our new allies, we parade the streets selling our newly found answers to the rest of society.

But in the midst of all of this chaos, there remains a group of people who are using their energy to overcome their adversities. These people are consumed with a passion for life—for enhancing their health, their happiness, and their productivity. These are the miracle makers. They use powerful strategies to solve their immediate problems.

We would be wise to study their efforts. We would be wise to consider their solutions. If we practiced what they practiced, we might find our own personal lives more enriched and rewarding.

Our miracle makers employed a variety of thinking strategies. They focused inward and paid attention to what they were saying to themselves and then they challenged those words. They rearranged their thoughts, shifted their beliefs, talked to themselves differently—they carried on a personal debate until they wrestled their "stinking thinking" to the ground. Once they shook up their minds, they were then prepared to change their lives. The new thinking was marked by a heightened enthusiasm, greater motivation, and stronger inspiration to make their lives better.

According to our miracle makers, they originally dedicated themselves to thinking that placed them in a personal mess and kept them there—fate had no right to do this to me, I can't survive without support, I'll change tomorrow, I'll never have a meaningful relationship, no one loves or cares for me.

Then these miracle makers changed their thinking around. They created a different perspective on life. They came to see a better way of approaching their personal adversities. They engaged in healthier thinking and looked at their challenges from a new angle—I can create a meaningful life even with my limitations, I must seize the opportunity and get on with life, I will not devote myself to worry but will devote myself to living, I appreciate my other strengths, this is my problem and I am committed to making positive changes now.

The question remains: if you had an opportunity to commit yourself to a particular line of thinking and reasoning, which one would it be? Again, the answer is obvious—the latter! The latter thinking—loaded with reason, logic, flexibility, patience, acceptance, optimism—is what propelled these miracle makers into creating their own miracles. No doubt a lot of hard work was involved, but underlying the hard work was a particular line of reasoning. This thinking separates the miracle makers from the rest of us. However, this thinking is also available to the rest of us. Once we dedicate ourselves to it, we will begin to notice our health, our happiness, and our productivity improve. And once these improve, we are well on our way to becoming our own personal miracle makers.

226

Epilogue _____

It is hoped that this book has been an adventure for you. Were some of your traditional views, values, and ideas about health, happiness, and productivity—and how to get them—challenged? Did you come away with a greater sense of personal empowerment?

Overcoming adversity in the workplace, on the homefront, in one's personal life—each of the miracle makers who speak in this book has found a way to triumph over tribulation. The problems discussed were serious and universal.

The powerful message that comes through in every interview is focused on the process of thinking. The power of the mind. You've heard it before, but now you really know what it means. Taking advantage of the mind to maximize its full potential. The basic message is to rethink the way you think and to do so in a more constructive and health-enhancing fashion.

The potential positive influence of the mind has been increasingly re-searched, and fascinating results have been discovered by scientific disciplines such as Rational-Emotive Therapy, Cognitive-Behavior Therapy, Neuroen-docrinology, and Psychoimmunology. In addition, other remarkable trends have been occurring in our society. Athletes all over the world are being taught to think differently in order to perform better. We see it happening in baseball, football, track and field, hockey, figure skating, golf, tennis, skiing, and countless other sports. East Germany (now unified with West Germany), which is a small nation of athletes compared to other nations, has been quietly capitalizing on the use of mental conditioning for a number of decades. Per capita East Germany won more gold medals during the summer Olympics than the United States and Canada combined. North American coaches in various training centers have finally hired sports psychologists to teach their athletes performance-enhancing thinking so that they can catch up.

On another front, patients are being instructed to think differently and are able to increase the production of "killer T-cells," which are vital physio-logical defense mechanisms in the battle against certain ailments including cancer. Additionally, cognitive restructuring procedures have been used with patients to overcome depression, anxiety, and anger.

If you're a movie buff you will surely remember the "Star Wars" trilogy. Reference to the absolute power of the mind was evident in the encouragement offered to Luke Skywalker: "May the force be with you." Frank Herbert, author of the highly acclaimed science fiction book series *Dune*, constantly wrote about the "force within us." Surely there exists a mental capacity within all of us that can enhance our health, happiness, and productivity.

I hope that it is becoming obvious that the way we think, the way we use our minds, weakens our ability or strengthens our ability to deal with problems. Our immune system is affected by how we think; our problem-solving abilities are influenced by how we think; our emotions are swayed by how we think. In short, how we think has a direct impact on every facet of our lives—our health, happiness, and productivity.

We don't have to regularly ruin our lives just because our lives seem to be in ruins! There are some key questions that you need to ask yourself in order to determine whether you are prepared to become a miracle maker.

Are you committed to your health, happiness, and productivity? Are you prepared to tolerate and accept unpredictability and uncertainty? Are you prepared to consider the real possibility that you have at least partly interfered with your ability to overcome your adversity? Are you willing to accept that you may not completely and totally overcome your adversity? Are you prepared to rethink the way your think? Once you truthfully declare yes to each of these questions, then you may be ready for the exciting journey awaiting you—the journey to self-discovery and self-empowerment.

ESSENTIAL QUALITIES OF A MIRACLE MAKER

There are some key characteristics and qualities that truly separate the miracle maker from other individuals.

First, the miracle maker takes responsibility for adversity, but does not take the blame. There is no point in blaming yourself for the mess that you are in. If you invest energy, time, and effort in blaming yourself, that will leave little in the way of resources required to take responsibility for the problem—and then eventually resolve it.

Second, the miracle maker has an extraordinary tolerance for ambiguity and unpredictability. As it is virtually impossible to anticipate when adversity will strike, it makes sense to build up your level of tolerance for that which "hath no rhymne or reason."

Third, this miracle maker maintains an ongoing acceptance of his or her limitations and frailties. It is very easy to condemn yourself for who you are not or what you do not have, but if instead you acknowledge and accept your shortcomings, you can then free up your energy for the work needed to make life better.

Fourth, the miracle maker sustains a strong acceptance of others' idiosyncrasies. It is tempting to blame others for our misery, but what does it really accomplish? Acknowledgment and acceptance of individual differences is a liberating quality, because you no longer are caught up in anger and blame. This does not necessarily mean that you have to like what others do, but if you don't get stuck in a destructive cycle of blame, you will have the time and energy to constructively challenge their ways.

Fifth, a burning and passionate commitment to help oneself and make things better is probably the most powerful quality of the miracle maker. Dedication and fierce devotion are needed to improve things so you can live a healthier, happier, and more productive life.

Finally, the miracle maker has an ongoing desire to develop and evolve these problem-management skills. No doubt practicing, rehearsing, upgrading, and expanding your abilities are essential to ensure that you stay on top of your problems.

If you can appreciate these qualities and characteristics and begin to practice these behaviors, then you will be able to develop your own adversity inoculation program. Once you become a powerful master of your own thinking, as these miracle makers seem to be, then you will be ready to challenge the negative influences that adversity can bring to bear on your life.

The mind is an important tool, but this rich network of thoughts and ideas cannot necessarily provide a universal remedy. Nonetheless, if you commit yourself to using your mind in a way that you have never used it before, in a new productive and flexible way, you will achieve the best possible quality of life under adverse conditions. That is really what this book has been all about. Easier said than done? Absolutely. But, as these miracle makers so clearly demonstrate, a better life is possible, indeed probable, if you make the effort.

OUR LIFE IS WHAT OUR THOUGHTS MAKE IT (Marcus Aurelius, ''Meditations'')

Bibliography ————————————

Beck, A.T., *Cognitive Therapies and Emotional Disorders*, New York, International University Press, 1976.

Borysenko, J., *Minding The Body, Mending The Mind*, Reading, Massachusetts, Addison-Wesley, 1987.

Cousins, N., *Anatomy Of An Illness*, New York, Bantam, 1981.

Ellis, A., *How To Stubbornly Refuse To Make Yourself Miserable About Anything Yes Anything*, New Jersey, Lyle Stuart Inc., 1988.

Ellis, A., *Overcoming Resistance: Rational Emotive Therapy With Difficult Clients*, New York, Springer, 1985.

Ellis, A. and Becker, I., *A Guide To Personal Happiness*, North Hollywood, California, Wilshire Books, 1982.

Ellis, A. and Knaus, W., *Overcoming Procrastination*, New York, New American Library, 1977.

Ellis, A., *Anger: How To Live With And Without It*, New Jersey, Citadel Press, 1977.

Ellis, A. and Harper, R.A., *A New Guide To Rational Living*, North Hollywood, California, Wilshire Books, 1975.

Ellis, A., *Techniques For Disputing Irrational Beliefs*, New York, Institute For Rational Emotive Therapy, 1974.

Ellis, A., *Humanistic Psychotherapy: The Rational-Emotive Approach*, New York, McGraw Hill, 1973.

Ellis, A., *Executive Leadership: A Rational Approach*, New York, Institute For Rational-Emotive Therapy, 1972.

Ellis, A., *Growth Through Reason*, North Hollywood, California, Wilshire Books, 1971.

Ellis, A., et al, *How To Raise An Emotionally Healthy, Happy Child*, North Hollywood, California, Wilshire Books, 1966.

Ellis, A., *Rational-Emotive Psychotherapy*, New York, Institute For Rational-Emotive Therapy, 1963.

Ellis, A. and Harper, R.A., *A Guide To Successful Marriage*, North Hollywood, California, Wilshire Books, 1961.

Klarreich, S., *Work Without Stress*, New York, Brunner/Mazel Publishers, 1990.

Klarreich, S., *Health And Fitness In The Workplace: Health Education In Business Organizations*, New York, Praeger, 1987.

Langer, E.J., *Mindfulness*, Reading, Massachusetts, Addison-Wesley, 1989.

Lazarus, R.S. and Folkman, S., *Stress Appraisal And Coping*, New York, Springer, 1984.

Lazarus, R.S., *Psychological Stress And The Coping Process*, New York, McGraw Hill, 1966.

Meichenbaum, D. and Jaremko, M.E., EDS., *Stress Reduction And Prevention*, New York, Plenum, 1983.

Pelletier, K.R., *Healthy People In Unhealthy Places*, Monterey, California, Merloyd Lawrence, 1984.

Simonton, O.C., et al, *Getting Well Again*, Los Angeles, Tarcher, 1978.